Since Babylon

Since Babylon

A Window on Israel from the Silent Years to 70 CE

ALLEN P. STOUFFER

RESOURCE *Publications* · Eugene, Oregon

SINCE BABYLON
A Window on Israel from the Silent Years to 70 CE

Copyright © 2022 Allen P. Stouffer. All rights reserved. Except for brief quotations in critical publications or reviews, no part of this book may be reproduced in any manner without prior written permission from the publisher. Write: Permissions, Wipf and Stock Publishers, 199 W. 8th Ave., Suite 3, Eugene, OR 97401.

Resource Publications
An Imprint of Wipf and Stock Publishers
199 W. 8th Ave., Suite 3
Eugene, OR 97401

www.wipfandstock.com

PAPERBACK ISBN: 978-1-6667-3214-6
HARDCOVER ISBN: 978-1-6667-2549-0
EBOOK ISBN: 978-1-6667-2550-6

05/25/22

Scripture quotations are taken from the New Revised Standard Version Bible, copyright © 1989 the Division of Christian Education of the National Council of the Churches of Christ in the United States of America. Used by permission. All rights reserved.

For Sarah

Contents

Preface | ix
Acknowledgments | xi
Introduction | xiii

I   Return from Babylon | 1
II   Alexander, the Ptolemies, and the Seleucids | 14
III   Jews Meet Greeks | 19
IV   Antiochus Epiphanes, the Abomination of Desolation, and the Maccabean Rebellion | 27
V   The Hasmonean Kingdom | 41
VI   The Romans: Pompey, Julius Caesar, Mark Antony, and Octavian | 45
VII   Herod | 52
VIII After Herod | 79
IX   Prefects and Procurators | 82
X   Reprise and Finale | 99
XI   Reflection | 111

Questions for Focus and Discussion | 125
Ancient Israel Timeline | 133
Hasmonean Dynasty | 134
Herod the Great's Family | 135
Bibliography | 137
Index | 139

Preface

ACCOMMODATIONS MADE IN BECOMING acclimatized to the workplace during life's early stages can leave a permanent imprint on one's future. Imperceptibly, they impose routines that slowly harden into lifelong patterns. Such was my experience during my working years. Classes had to be prepared, essays and exams marked, meetings attended and minutes recorded, and reference letters written; research was ongoing, and there was a never-ending list of articles and new books to be digested—all the normal features of life in academia. Family life, with my wife and our two sons, brought the usual domestic responsibilities that competed for attention with social events and exercise time, and there were regular church obligations. One hoped for some creative relaxation with a hobby, if any time remained. In many respects it was a praiseworthy schedule, replete with admirable activities, yet, in retrospect, a crucial element was missing; it allotted no space to ordered Bible study and spiritual reflection. In retirement I resolved to end this neglect.

To remedy this situation, I decided to learn what books seminaries were using to introduce their students to biblical studies. After considerable searching, I chose two—*Old Testament Survey: The Message, Form, and Background of the Old Testament*, second edition, by LaSor, Hubbard, and Bush, and *Introducing the New Testament: Its Literature and Theology*, by Achtemeier, Green, and Thompson—and began working through them slowly and systematically. This broad examination of the Bible was by no means wholly new territory, for my undergraduate double major was in biblical literature and history. History was the focus of my professional life, however, and the biblical material gradually receded far back into the remote recesses of my memory from forty years of inattention. It was almost like starting over again. As I engaged with this broad review of the Bible, it slowly dawned on me that there was a long passage of time between the end of the Old Testament's account of Israel's history and the Jews' reappearance in the New Testament text. Likely I had learned of this gap in the biblical story in my undergraduate biblical literature courses; if so, it had long since faded from memory. Perhaps it was my natural interest in social continuity as a historian that brought it to my attention. Whatever the reason, the obvious blank space in the biblical story captured my interest; I decided to learn what became of the Jews in the four centuries after their story disappears from the Old Testament canon.

It was a project I could now pursue at a leisurely pace. It continued for more than a decade. At one point I was scheduled to give an eight-week course on the topic to a group of interested adults in a church study group, but that was scuttled by cardiac surgery.

This piece is the project's outcome. Hopefully it will be informative for lay persons interested in the history of the ancient Jews, their faith ancestors, during the Old Testament's silent years.

Acknowledgments

DURING THIS PROJECT'S LENGTHY gestation, judicious input came from several sources. I am especially indebted to James McDowell for his encouragement, support, and penetrating insight. The theological discussion group we both belong to read and discussed an early draft at his suggestion, and the issues considered in its sessions helped to set the piece's ultimate course. Later, his keen editorial sense identified wrinkles in the wording where awkward prose obscured the intended meaning. In addition, he saw that providing a timeline for ancient Israel would be beneficial for readers.

Dr. John Sider, Westmont College Distinguished Professor Emeritus, offered constructive advice on a later draft and recommended adding visual representations on the Hasmonean dynasty and Herod the Great's family. Retired Anglican Rector Ross Gill's assessment emphasized its potential as background reading for fellowship/Bible study groups preparing to study the Gospels.

Our two sons were generous with their technical knowledge. Scott prepared the charts for the appendix, while on occasion Kirk rescued me from computerland's bewildering labyrinths. But without my wife Sarah's patient and ongoing encouragement, the piece would have remained no more than an idea. She believed in it from the beginning, and persevered in urging me to consider a book.

I also wish to thank all at Resource Publications, especially Matthew Wimer, George and Emily Callihan, and my editor, Griffin Edwards, for their cordial manner and efficient ways in supporting this project's completion.

Introduction

THE OLD TESTAMENT IS a rich source of information about ancient Israel. For a significant portion of early Israel's past, it is virtually the only source. The account begins when God asks Abram to leave his native Ur for an uncertain destination. It records the establishment of the covenant with Abram and his descendants, before following the patriarchs Isaac, Jacob, and Joseph to the Israelites' time in Egypt. The story continues with Moses leading the exodus from the Nile Valley, the giving of the law and the covenant's extension to the twelve tribes at Sinai, and their entry into Canaan, where judges rule for a time. Around the beginning of the first millennium BCE David unites the twelve tribes into the kingdom of Israel with its capital at Jerusalem. Solomon, his successor, using conscripted labor, raises the city's status by building the temple, the focal point of national life. Solomon's forceful methods prove costly, however, for when Rehoboam, his successor, continues his father's strong-handed ways, the northern tribes secede under Jeroboam's leadership, and the kingdom divides late in the tenth century. An Assyrian invasion decimates the northern kingdom in the late eighth century, and many of its citizens are dispersed throughout Assyria, and replaced with settlers from the conquering power. Early in the sixth century the Babylonians invade Judea, destroy the temple and much of Jerusalem, and exile many leading Judeans to Babylon. Seventy years later the Persians defeat Babylon and permit the Judean expatriates to return. With Persian support they reoccupy Jerusalem and rebuild the temple and the city wall, but the monarchy is not restored, and Judea remains part of Persia's "Province Beyond the River" until late in the fourth century. This, in brief, is the broad outline of ancient Israel's history from its earliest antiquity to the late fifth century, as it appears in the Old Testament.

Introduction

Some question a segment of the Old Testament narrative's historicity. Biblical minimalists tend to see the patriarchs from Abraham to Moses as eponymous heroes—mythical figures—akin to the medieval giants Gargantua and Pantagruel, the legendary Celtic King Arthur, or Robin Hood and Paul Bunyan. Michael Grant, for example, finds the patriarchal narrative so "anachronistic and inconsistent" as to raise doubts that the patriarchs "ever existed at all—just as Agamemnon and Menelaus, of Greek mythology, may never have existed."[1] Martin Noth begins his authoritative *History of Israel* only as the twelve tribes occupy Palestine.[2] Alberto Soggin, dismissing the patriarchal account as romanticized and unhistorical, opens his 1984 survey of Israel's history with the united kingdom when, in his view, the story contains enough economic and political detail to avoid suspicion of being the product of later writers' imagination.[3]

Scholars with a high view of Scripture discredit the minimalists' claim that the Old Testament patriarchal narrative is heroic legend. They understand the biblical account to be uniquely inspired by the Holy Spirit, in which God reveals himself in the record of his interaction with the Hebrew people, through whom he chose to channel his revelation. A recent book by Iain Provan, Philips Long, and Tremper Longman, entitled *A Biblical History of Israel*, questions the minimalists' reasons for doubting the Old Testament patriarchal narrative. The study finds the minimalists' choice of dates before which to reject the biblical account's reliability to be arbitrary and defends the Old Testament's historicity.[4]

While differing on the patriarchal narrative's historicity, Old Testament scholars close ranks on the biblical account's reliability from the united kingdom to the close of the Judeans' homeward migration from Babylon late in the fifth century, where the Old Testament history of ancient Israel ends with the Ezra/Nehemiah story. This leaves a four-hundred-year gap in the canonical record, until the Jews resurface in the first-century-CE New Testament text. It contains little information about Israel's final days, however, when the temple is destroyed in the First Roman War late in the first century, for the text focuses on Jesus' life and his followers' activities.

The four-century lacuna in the biblical record of the Jews—a considerable span, roughly equaling the time from the arrival of the first European

1. Grant, *History of Ancient Israel*, 30.
2. Noth, *History of Israel*, 5–6.
3. Soggin, *History of Ancient Israel*, 21–31.
4. Provan et al., *Biblical History of Israel*, 3–9, 13–18.

Introduction

settlers in North America to the present—is puzzling. Christians believe that God chose the Israelites to be the channel for revealing himself to humans, yet the Old Testament unaccountably leaves the story unfinished. Because of the biblical canon's silence, this period, extending from the Jews' return from Babylon to their reappearance in the New Testament text, has become known as the "Silent Years." Lay Christians tend to gloss over this lengthy interstice in the biblical account, largely, it seems, because they are unaware of it, for many learned their history of ancient Israel from the Old Testament.

This work presents a general narrative account of Israel's history during the Silent Years. It is directed to curious laypersons interested in learning what became of Israel after it disappeared from the Old Testament record. To establish context, it begins by surveying the geopolitical landscape in the eastern Mediterranean and the Middle East as the Judeans return from the Babylonian captivity, during the last third of the sixth century BCE and the first two-thirds of the fifth century. It traces Israel's history as a vassal nation successively of the Persians, the Ptolemies, and the Seleucids, until the Judeans recover their independence briefly under the Maccabees, only to be reduced to a client kingdom, and then a province of the Roman Empire, giving particular attention to Greek culture's impact on Israel.

The Silent Years end with the death of Israel's king Herod, but concluding this study there would disregard the fact that Israel is then at the peak of its splendor, wealth, and territorial extent since the glory days of David and Solomon. Accordingly, to complete ancient Israel's story, the study continues into the late first century CE, when Israel is finally destroyed in the First Roman War. Beyond offering a window on the Jews' history after they disappear from the Old Testament narrative, this builds a bridge connecting the Old and New Testaments. Additionally, it sheds light on the context in which the events of the New Testament occurred and the Christian church was born. The writer also believes there may be timely instruction for perceptive twenty-first-century Christians in Israel's encounter with Hellenism during the Silent Years.

I

Return from Babylon

To set the stage, it is necessary to establish the historical context by examining the geopolitical contours of the Middle East and the eastern Mediterranean as the Judean exiles returned to Palestine. This migration continued for an extended period in the late sixth and fifth centuries BCE. In 559 Cyrus (559–30),[1] the future Persian emperor, seized power among the south Persian tribes, and Persia grew quickly under his leadership. Within a decade he controlled all the neighboring lands from the Persian Gulf to the Halys River in Asia Minor (present-day Turkey). Three years later he defeated King Croesus of Lydia, who controlled the western half of Asia Minor, and extended Persian influence to the shores of the Aegean Sea. In 539 he took Mesopotamia from the Babylonians after defeating Belshazzar. Cambyses (529–22), his successor, added Egypt in 525, and Darius (521–486) consolidated and organized the empire by dividing it into administrative provinces called satrapies. A great builder, Darius dug a canal connecting the Nile River with the Red Sea, laid the great Royal Road across the empire from Susa to Sardis, and built the new city of Persepolis. Persia was the power dominating the Middle East as the Jews returned to their homeland in Judea, a small sub-district in the Persian satrapy of "the Province Beyond the River."

1. Dates in parentheses after names denote the reigns of figures unless otherwise noted.

Since Babylon

In the eastern Mediterranean Greece was the great power. It was not a country with a central government like Persia, but consisted of numerous city-states—independent cities, governed by citizen assemblies that controlled the adjacent territory. The Greeks dominated the Aegean Sea, and had colonies scattered along its eastern shores (Ionia), around the neighboring Black Sea, and as far west as southern Italy, southern France, and Spain. Socrates, Plato, and Aristotle were its great philosophers, and its historians, Herodotus and Thucydides, laid the foundations of historical writing. The Greeks were the first people in the ancient world to offer rational, rather than supernatural, explanations of phenomena in the physical order, and in this respect their outlook was remarkably modern. They also were known for their athletic prowess, symbolized by the Olympic Games they founded, and twenty-first-century theaters still stage Greek plays. Their civilization reached its apex in the fifth century BCE, the age of Pericles, the great Athenian. They founded a civilization that had a far-reaching influence in shaping the culture of the Western world.

Given their proximity, strife between Persia and Greece was virtually inevitable. The die was cast for a clash when Cyrus defeated Croesus, king of Lydia, a state in western Asia Minor, in 546, for this gave the Persians access to the eastern shore of the Aegean Sea and the Greek colonies in Ionia. Conflict erupted in 499, when the Ionian colonies began to resist Persian influence, for the Greek city-states under Athenian leadership came to the Ionians' aid. To punish the Greeks for assisting them, Darius sent a large army to the Greek mainland. With great effort the Greeks defeated the Persians at the Battle of Marathon in eastern Attica opposite Athens in 490. A decade later the Persians sought revenge for this loss. Xerxes (485–65), Darius's successor, sent a fleet of six hundred ships and an army of one hundred and fifty thousand overland to invade Greece. In a naval encounter near an island off the west coast of Attica—the Battle of Salamis in 480—the Greeks defeated the Persian fleet, which had to withdraw. The following year, after a decisive loss at the Battle of Platea a short distance northwest of Athens, their intended objective, the Persians abandoned their efforts to add Greece to their empire. Had the Persians prevailed in their expansionist policy, the West's future might have been quite different. Asian civilization, with its despotic political traditions, might have spread to Europe. Their victory would have stifled Greek civilization, where the seeds of democracy were germinating, and Western civilization might have developed in a very different direction. As the Jews began returning to Judea in the late sixth century following their Babylonian captivity, they encountered a world in which Greece and Persia were competing for dominance. The winner would have a significant impact on their future.

Their migration began in 539 or 538, after Cyrus defeated Belshazzar, the king of Babylon, where the Judeans had been exiled. Cyrus added the captured Babylonian Empire, which included the areas that previously had been the kingdoms of Judah and Israel, to the Persian satrapy called the Province Beyond the River. He decreed the Judeans' release, clearing the way for their homeward movement to begin, a lengthy migration that continued for more than a century.

The closing verses of Second Chronicles begin the story, which continues in the first six chapters of Ezra.[2] The latter account says the Lord prompted Cyrus to build a house for him in Jerusalem, and Cyrus issued a decree in 539 inviting any Judean exiles so disposed to return to Jerusalem and undertake the task. Cyrus's policy was unusual, for customarily Eastern rulers dispersed inhabitants of lands they conquered to facilitate governing the newly acquired regions. The victorious Assyrians had relocated the ten northern tribes throughout their empire, while King Nebuchadnezzar of Babylon sent the Judeans to his homeland. By allowing the Judeans to return home, Cyrus indicated his intention to rule them with a gentler hand, and the Judeans were destined to experience a large measure of autonomy in their homeland under Persian suzerainty.

Cyrus appointed Sheshbazzar, son of former Judean King Jehoiachin and thus a prince of Judah, to lead the expedition and be governor of the homeland. The exiles' neighbors were instructed to assist the returnees with money and goods, and gold vessels Nebuchadnezzar had seized from the temple seventy years earlier were entrusted to Sheshbazzar for transport to Jerusalem. The journey occurred sometime in 538. The migrants reportedly laid the temple's foundation, a claim also attributed to a later body of returnees, but failed to accomplish their main objective—rebuilding the temple. No more is heard of Sheshbazzar, and he disappears from the biblical record.[3]

A second return migration occurred about two decades later. Led by Zerubbabel, another Judean prince and grandson of Jehoiachin, it must have taken place about 520, for Haggai's prophecies to Zerubbabel urging the rebuilding of the temple occurred in the second year of Darius's reign. Zerubbabel was appointed governor of Judea either by Darius or his predecessor

---

2. Grant, *History of Ancient Israel*, 181; 2 Chr 36:22–24; Ezra 1–6.
3. Ezra 1:1–11, 5:14–16, LaSor et al., *Old Testament Survey*, 392.

Cambyses, who ruled from 530 to 522. Soon after the expedition arrived the high priest Jeshua, who accompanied Zerubbabel, reconstructed the altar, a structure of vital importance, for it facilitated the reinstatement of the sacrificial ritual central to Israel's religious-life-long practices in the temple.[4]

The returnees' attention then turned to rebuilding the temple, a matter in which interest had lagged. The prophets Haggai and Zechariah played a key role in this. Why should Jerusalem's residents live in the comfort of "paneled houses," Haggai asked, when the Lord's house remained unbuilt? His appeal stirred Zerubbabel and Jeshua into action. They placed the rebuilding task's direction in the Levites' hands.[5]

When the work began, however, it reignited long-smoldering opposition to the temple's reconstruction among the neighboring residents of Samaria. These people were the descendants of the Assyrian settlers who had replaced the ten northern tribes banished to Assyria several centuries earlier. This opposition, which included bribing officials, had been encountered by the exiles who returned with Sheshbazzar, and likely explains why they failed to rebuild the temple. When Zerubbabel's builders began work on the foundation, the opponents offered to help, saying, "We worship your God as you do, and we have been sacrificing to him since the days of Esar-haddon [681–68] who brought us here." Zerubbabel, probably questioning their real motives, rejected the offer, insisting that the returned Judeans would rebuild the temple themselves, as directed by Cyrus's original decree. He may also have feared losing control of the project if the Samaritans participated.[6]

Zerubbabel's opponents, however, refused to drop the matter. Led by Tattenai, governor of the Province Beyond the River, and his assistant Shetharbozenai, they challenged Zerubbabel, asking by whose authority he was rebuilding the temple. When he replied that it was by Cyrus's decree, Tattenai appealed to Darius, the current king, who had come to Persia's throne in 521, for confirmation of Zerubbabel's claim. Given the lapse of more than two decades, the Persians evidently had forgotten the earlier decree, for it required a search of the royal archives for court officials to find Cyrus's original directive, with its detailed instructions for the temple's construction. Darius peremptorily ordered Tattenai and his compatriots to stay away from Jerusalem, pay the building costs from provincial revenues "without delay," and supply whatever the priests needed to carry on temple sacrifices "day by

4. LaSor et al., *Old Testament Survey*, 392, endnotes 11, 12; Hag 1:1; Ezra 3:1–6.
5. Hag 1; Ezra 1:2–3, 8–11, 5:1–2.
6. Ezra 4:1–4.

day without fail." Tattenai promptly complied, and this, the Second Temple, was completed in 515 and dedicated with great celebration.[7]

Half a century later, in 457, the seventh year of the Persian king Artaxerxes's reign (464–24), there was a third homecoming. Ezra, the expedition's leader, was given royal instructions authorizing the expedition and permitting other Judeans to accompany him. Artaxerxes underwrote it and sent money for offerings in Jerusalem and vessels for the temple. Ezra's instructions directed the king's treasurers in the Province Beyond the River to help him acquire whatever he needed, up to a value of one hundred silver talents, and exempted priests from taxation. Artaxerxes, it seems, hoped to gain the goodwill of his Israelite subjects. Before departing Ezra gathered the returnees to pray and fast for three days. The journey took four months, and on arriving the Judeans offered burnt offerings, delivered the vessels to the temple, and presented Artaxerxes's orders to the provincial officials.[8]

Ezra's mission, however, involved more than leading a band of exiled Judeans home like Sheshbazzar and Zerubbabel. The biblical narrative describes Ezra as a "scribe skilled in the law of Moses" who "had set his heart to study the law of the Lord, and do it, and to teach the statutes and ordinances in Israel." Artaxerxes's instructions directed him to teach the laws of God, and as well the laws of the king, to those ignorant of them, and to appoint magistrates to implement them in the Province Beyond the River. Ezra's mission thus had a spiritual as well as a political dimension.[9]

Soon after arriving, Ezra learned that the earlier returnees, including the priests and Levites, had intermarried with the non-Jewish people. This grieved him deeply, for, as one learned in the law, he would have known that Moses had sternly admonished the Israelites not to intermarry with the Canaanites. This, Moses had warned, would turn their children away from Jehovah to worship other gods. Appalled that the people had violated Moses' instruction, Ezra took drastic action to correct the situation. He fasted and prayed and publicly confessed the people's sins before God. This brought out a large gathering of the people, who acknowledged their sin in the matter. They agreed to send away the "foreign" wives and their children. To oversee this task, judges were appointed to question the people and identify those who had married foreign women. Any who failed to appear for questioning were to lose their property and be banned from

7. Ezra 5:1–6—6:17.
8. Ezra 7–8.
9. Ezra 7:6, 10.

the congregation of returned exiles. The interviews took two months, and when they were completed the wives and children were banished.[10]

Ezra's severe measure seemingly awakened the people's interest in the law, for on the first day of the month they assembled and asked him to read them the law. The reading continued daily for a week, accompanied with explanation and commentary so that the people could understand it. This implies that the people were ignorant of the law, so it was a vital learning experience for them.

They learned that Moses had instituted the Festival of Booths, which was to be celebrated yearly for a week in the seventh month. The first day was to be a "holy convocation" when no work was done. The people were to live in booths made of tree branches—temporary shelters—for a week while the law was read. The festival's purpose was to remind the Israelites that God had made them live in booths during the exodus from Egypt. Having learned this, Ezra had the returnees gather branches from which they made booths in which they lived for the seven days as the law was being read. On the eighth day there was a solemn assembly, as Moses' law required. Thus, following the banishment of the foreign wives, Ezra reinstated the Festival of Booths, which the people had not celebrated since Joshua's time[11]

This intensive week-long study of the law, as Ezra reinstated the Festival of Booths, profoundly affected the Judean returnees. Having lived far from Jerusalem, where there was no temple for two or three generations, most never would have witnessed the law's sacrificial rituals. Collective knowledge of the law's details would have dimmed. Memory of their history—Egyptian slavery, the exodus and God's provision for their needs during the forty wilderness years, reception of the Ten Commandments and the covenant at Sinai, divine help in occupying Canaan, the establishment of the kingdom, prosperity and peace when they obeyed the law, punishment and hardship when they ignored it—would have faded, for the law's rituals were intended in part to remind them of their past. When they rediscovered all of this from hearing the law read, it was a humbling learning experience.

It produced a dramatic affect. After separating themselves from the "foreigners" in their midst, they publicly confessed their sin in sackcloth and ashes, and recalled the iniquitous behavior of their ancestors. Ezra addressed God in a lengthy public prayer, acknowledging God's forbearance

---

10. Ezra 9:5–15, 10:7–44.
11. Lev 23:33–36, 39–44; Deut 31:10–13; Neh 8:1–18.

and loving care despite Israel's long history of reprehensible behavior, which had justly brought them to their present condition. He beseeched God to "not treat lightly" the Judeans' present deplorable plight that found them slaves in the land he had given their ancestors. "Its yield goes to the king you have set over us because of our sins," he lamented; "they have power also over our bodies" and "we are in great distress." In response, the people formally resolved to keep the law. They prepared a document to that affect, which the public officials, priests, and Levites signed. It committed them to "walk in God's law, which was given by Moses the servant of God, and to observe and do all the commandments of the Lord our Lord and his ordinances and statutes." This was a momentous step, amounting to a renewal of the covenant agreed to at Sinai.[12]

Although many exiles had returned to Judea and the temple was rebuilt, surprisingly, the city of Jerusalem itself remained in the ruined state the early-sixth-century Babylonian attack had left it. In 444 a visitor to Susa, the Persian capital, from Judea reported that descendants of those Jews who had avoided removal to Babylon were in "great trouble," and Jerusalem's broken wall and burned gates had not been repaired since the days of Nebuchadnezzar. The text doesn't specify the nature of the home-staying Judeans' "great trouble," but this news greatly saddened Nehemiah, a Judean exile still in Babylon who was King Artaxerxes's cupbearer. In the ancient world palace intrigue was a constant threat for royal households. The office of cupbearer was an important post, for the cupbearer guarded the king from being poisoned by overseeing the royal table's food and drink, even to the point of sampling it himself. Constantly in the king's presence and privy to secret information, he had to be entirely trustworthy and a source of honest counsel. Grief-stricken at his countrymen's deplorable condition, Nehemiah fasted and prayed and then approached the king for help. Artaxerxes responded warmly to Nehemiah's appeal. Evidently believing that Nehemiah was capable of being a strong leader, the king appointed him governor of Judea with authority to go to Jerusalem and repair the city. He sent Nehemiah on his way with a royal escort, written authorization for his passage to the Province Beyond the River, and instructions directing the royal forester to provide timber for rebuilding purposes.[13]

On arriving in Jerusalem Nehemiah inspected the city's ruined walls and burned gates. He wisely appealed to residents' civic pride by challenging

---

12. Neh 9, 10:1–39.
13. Neh 1:1—2:8, 5:14.

them to end the disgrace of living in Israel's once-proud city with mounds of rubbish for walls and gates that were burned. After telling them of God's approval and Artaxerxes's generosity, he won their support, and they agreed to rebuild the wall. Assuming, undoubtedly, that some competition would facilitate the project, he shrewdly organized the work by assigning families and groups to build sections or gates.[14]

Like Zerubbabel, Nehemiah encountered opposition when he began rebuilding. On learning that someone from Susa concerned about the Judeans' wellbeing had arrived in Jerusalem, it alarmed Samarian governor Sanballat and Tobiah, governor of neighboring Ammon. As imperial officials, they may have suspected that Nehemiah was a trusted royal emissary sent by the court to investigate the management of Judean affairs. If so, it might signal similar investigations for the whole of the Province Beyond the River, an unsettling prospect for the two neighboring governors. On the other hand, perhaps jealousy motivated them, for Artaxerxes had underwritten Nehemiah's expedition, and he had arrived accompanied by a royal escort, with imperial money for temple sacrifices, and instructions requiring local officials to give him substantial support. Such favorable treatment would have marked Nehemiah as the king's favorite, and would not have escaped Sanballat and Tobiah's attention.[15]

When Sanballat saw the people beginning to work at the wall, he tauntingly asked his friends and army officers if these "feeble Jews" could really rebuild it from a pile of rubbish. Tobiah ridiculed it for being so weak that if crossed by a fox it would fall down. However, when the governors saw the wall continuing to rise, their opposition hardened, and they talked of attacking. These rumors soon spread among the Jews, who repeatedly warned Nehemiah of an imminent raid. Conditions became menacing, for not only was there the threat of an impending attack, but the great quantity of decades-old detritus was impeding construction, and the laborers were tiring. Unintimidated, Nehemiah resolutely armed the workers, rallying them with a reminder of God's might and greatness and a patriotic call to be prepared to fight for their homes and families. After Sanballat and Tobiah learned that their plot had been discovered, however, they refrained from attacking. The building continued, with half the laborers armed and

---

14. Neh 2:11—3:1-32.
15. Provan et al., *Biblical History of Israel*, 301; Neh 2:9-10.

standing guard while the others continued to build with swords strapped to their sides.[16]

When the wall was finished but before thegates were replaced, Sanballat and Tobiah made a final effort to sabotage the construction. They asked Nehemiah to meet them in a village outside Jerusalem. Suspecting that they intended to harm if not kill him, he wisely refused. After several more invitations were extended and rejected, the two governors threatened to make serious trouble for Nehemiah at the royal court if he did not comply. They informed him of rumors that the Jews had rebuilt the wall because they intended to rebel against the Persian Empire and make him king of Judea. Should this word reach Susa, they warned, he would be charged with treason. Not intimidated, Nehemiah calmly replied that the claim was nothing more than the product of the governors' over-heated imaginations, who were trying to frighten the Judeans into abandoning the project. Undeterred by the thinly-veiled threat, Nehemiah pressed on with the work, and the construction was completed in fifty-two days.[17] He thus achieved the primary objective that had brought him to Judea and confirmed King Artaxerxes's confidence in his leadership potential.

After holding a great celebration at the wall's dedication, Nehemiah concluded his work with two further steps. He remonstrated with local officials over commercial activity that was occurring on the Sabbath. This brought closure of Jerusalem's gates on the Sabbath so that no trade could enter the city and seemingly restored the Sabbath's sanctity. Despite Ezra's severe measures to stamp out intermarriage with Canaanites several decades early, it was continuing in Judea. Nehemiah vigorously opposed the practice until the people relented and took an oath to end it.[18]

Thus, as the Judean exiles resettled in their homeland, Persia and Greece, the region's great powers, were shaping the world they entered. Israel's part in that larger Persian-Greco world was a diminutive one, but the Jews were soon creating their own narrative, in which Zerubbabel and Nehemiah played supporting roles while Ezra was the protagonist. Zerubbabel led considerable numbers home to Judea, and despite substantial resistance rebuilt the temple, the centerpiece of national life. Nehemiah also overcame opposition to rebuild Jerusalem's wall and restore the Sabbath and revealed his ability as a great leader. Ezra, too, returned many to their

16. Neh 4:1–3, 6–23.
17. Neh 6:1–9, 15–16.
18. Neh 12:27–43, 13:15–30.

Judean homeland, but his main contribution was, as the second Moses, bringing the Jews back to the law and the covenant.

The agreement Nehemiah secured to end the practice of intermarriage with "foreign" people was the final event in the story of Israel's return from the Babylonian captivity. Surprisingly, it also brought an abrupt close to the entire Old Testament story of the Jews. That there should be such an inauspicious finish to the Old Testament's grand epic of the Hebrews, God's chosen people, is puzzling. After the exiles reach Judea, build the temple, restore the wall, and recommit to the law, the story simply ends. No summary or conclusion is offered, as one would expect with the conclusion of an historical account; instead, Scripture abandons Israel's story until the pages of the New Testament four centuries later. And even there, as we have seen, the text says virtually nothing about ancient Israel's final demise in the late first century CE. This raises significant questions about the Jews' existence in the intervening years. Did they continue to honor the law and the covenant, as they promised in Ezra's day? Or did they revert to the disobedient ways of their ancestors? And what became of the kingdom? Did Israel, God's select vehicle for revealing himself to humans, cease to exist, as a reader might conclude? Scripture offers no answers, and provides no explanation, for this ending of the Old Testament's narrative. The four-hundred-year-gap seems wholly incongruous with Israel's unique status, and the thoughtful reader is left to wonder.

Perhaps the responsibility for closing the story so unexpectedly with the Ezra/Nehemiah episode should be laid at the doorstep of those who selected which ancient writings to include in the Old Testament canon. Historical works from the intervening years by Jewish authors—the Books of the Maccabees, for example—might have been included. Were they omitted because the canon's compilers believed that nothing important enough to warrant inclusion happened during the era? Or, might it be that the biblical canon once contained writings on the Silent Years that were misplaced and ultimately disappeared, just as the law was lost sight of during the Babylonian captivity? While plausible, such explanations are problematic, for they fail to take into account the Christian belief in the Holy Spirit's participation in the preparation and preservation of Scripture. This points to the conclusion that the absence of Israel's narrative from the Old Testament during the Silent Years was not an oversight.

Light is thrown on this enigma if Scripture's purpose is recalled. Second Timothy declares that "All Scripture is inspired by God and is useful for teaching, for reproof, for correction and training in righteousness."[19] In other words, Scripture's purpose is twofold: teaching humans about God, and instructing them how to live.

As the Old Testament narrative unfolds, it reveals much about God's nature. He is the creator and a loving father who rescues his children from Egyptian slavery, provides for their physical needs in the wilderness, and helps them secure a homeland in Canaan. He is a righteous and jealous God, requiring ethical behavior and individual loyalty from his chosen people. A just God, he rewards uprightness and punishes sin, but is patient and forgiving in response to repentance. To be sure, the revelation is incomplete, for finite humans would be incapable of comprehending the full disclosure of an infinite deity, but the description of God's character is rich and more than adequate to instruct and satisfy humans.

At Sinai, as the Israelites prepare to enter Canaan and are about to assume the responsibilities of nationhood, they are given the Ten Commandments to serve as a model for guiding their behavior. Its first four directives specify how they are to relate to God. The remaining six are ethical rules for governing their relations with others. The original covenant, first given to Abraham, is extended to the Israelites, Abraham's descendants. God promises to protect and reward them with peace and long life if they honor the law. From the Old Testament thousand-year narrative the reader learns of Israel's successes and failures in complying with these imperatives in real-life circumstances. They experience prosperity and wellbeing when they honor the law, but harsh consequences follow when they disregard it. Their repeated delinquencies are clearly evident in the story. The reader cannot fail to see that divine involvement in human affairs is necessary if humans are to be redeemed from their disobedient ways. By Ezra and Nehemiah's time, the Old Testament narrative has fulfilled its instructional purpose for future readers if they are prepared to learn from it. The plot needs no further development. Having fulfilled its instructional purpose, the story can end.

If there is completeness in the Old Testament narrative, if enough of God's nature and what he expects of humans has been revealed to fulfill Scripture's instructional purpose, then believers may justifiably ask whether anything meaningful is to be gained/learned from examining the Jews' experience during the Silent Years. When the biblical canon is aphonic, why should Christians bother exploring Jewish history during the intertestamental years? The question is warranted.

---

19. 2 Tim 3:16.

Three reasons for doing so suggest themselves. The first is simply to satisfy curiosity. One learns much about Jewish history from the Old Testament up to the fourth century BCE and, as well, when the Jews resurface in the first-century-CE narrative, as the events recorded in the New Testament occur. It is only natural to wonder what happened to them during the intervening years, for obviously they did not cease to exist. Filling the historical knowledge gap about a people with whom Christians have a unique connection is a reasonable pursuit.

The second reason is contextual. The context in question is the first century CE, when the events recorded in the Gospels and the other books of the New Testament take place. Knowing the course of Jewish history during the intertestamental years informs the reader of the Jews' circumstances as the first century begins. This provides insight into the functioning of Jewish society and the forces shaping it at the time. It sets the stage, and illustrates the background, against which the New Testament unfolds. Equipped with this knowledge, the reader is better prepared to understand the text while working through the New Testament.

The third reason is a didactic one, for in learning about Jewish history during the Silent Years, there may be instruction for twenty-first-century believers. As we shall see, Greek culture entered Palestine during the intertestamental years. Some Jews welcomed it as a forward-looking progressive force, while others resisted its incorporation into Jewish life, believing it would lead Judean society away from the path inherent in the law they had agreed to follow. Greek culture became a disruptive influence that divided and weakened Jewish society. Inimical cultural forces also surround twenty-first-century believers; they may find knowing about the Jews' experience during the Silent Years to be relevant and instructive for their own circumstances.

During the century following Nehemiah's governorship (444–32)—from the reign of Darius II (424–04) to that of Darius III (336–30)—little is known of Judea's political life.[20] Judea remained a small sub-district of the Province Beyond the River, consisting of Jerusalem and a small strip of neighboring land: a quadrilateral about thirty-five miles long, stretching from Bethel in the north to Bethzur in the south, and the twenty-five-to-thirty-miles-wide plateau between the Dead Sea and the coastal lowlands, covering barely one thousand square miles. A Persian governor and

---

20. The Persian kings during the century following Nehemiah were Darius II Ochus, 424–04; Artaxerxes II Arsaces, 404–359; Artaxerxes III Ochus, 359–38; Artaxerxes IV Arces, 338–36; and Darius III Artashasta, 336–30. See Cartledge, *Alexander the Great*, 295.

financial officer resided in Jerusalem. Judeans, except for priests, Levites, and temple personnel, paid imperial taxes, and were subject to military service. However, like other subject peoples in the Persian Empire, they enjoyed a large measure of autonomy. As communal head, on coming to office the high priest was anointed and invested with royal trappings; he directed national affairs, serving under the authority of the Persian emperor. During the later years of Persian rule, in the reign of Artaxerxes III (359–38), stability around Jerusalem and Samaria declined. It stemmed from unrest in the neighboring Phoenician city-states who revolted, and the turbulence spread into Judea.[21] Meanwhile, in the larger Greco-Persian world, events were occurring that would greatly affect the Judeans.

---

21. Bickerman, *From Ezra to the Last of the Maccabees*, 11–13; Grant, *History of Ancient Israel*, 187, 190, 199.

II

Alexander, the Ptolemies, and the Seleucids

AS WE HAVE SEEN, the Persians, having suffered a devastating defeat at the hands of the Greeks in the Battle of Platea near Athens, abandoned their westward aspirations. However, war between the two powers—war that eventually impacted the Judeans—continued sporadically for a century and a half. To help defend against possible future Persian aggression, the Greek city-states and their Ionian countrymen formed the Delian League in 477. It was a defensive alliance, much like NATO, which the Atlantic powers organized following WWII; members contributed either money or ships. Initially headquartered on the Aegean Island of Delos, the League eventually moved to Athens, which came to dominate it. In time the other city-states resisted Athens's domination of the pact, bringing conflict that erupted into intermittent warfare for a century. Weakened by the ongoing struggle, the city-states were an easy prey for Macedon, Greece's fifth century-BCE northern neighbor and now mostly part of modern Greece. Philip, the Macedonian king, gained control of all the Greek city-states after defeating their combined forces at Chaeronea in 338, and then prepared to add Persia to his domain. He was assassinated in 336, however, before he could launch his campaign, but his son Alexander—Alexander the Great to future historians—succeeded him and implemented his father's foreign policy.

Alexander, the Ptolemies, and the Seleucids

A military genius, Alexander succeeded in vanquishing the Persians, and built a vast empire stretching twenty-five hundred miles across southwestern Asia to India in a mere dozen years. His success depended on a well-trained, highly disciplined professional army employing new methods. Unlike previous armies that relied on cumbersome, slow-moving supply trains for transport, Alexander's infantry moved quickly, for each soldier carried his own supplies. His army also used a new battle formation—the phalanx—in which soldiers, armed with long two-handed pikes, massed in squares sixteen rows deep and wide. Trained to wheel in step in any direction, they could double their front by filing off in rows of eight, enabling them to maneuver with great agility. His forces also formed intelligence units that gathered information about the enemy's plans and spread rumors and disinformation to confuse them. These tactics, and his rigorously disciplined soldiers, enabled Alexander to win victory after victory in his rapid eastward march across southwestern Asia.[1]

Alexander crossed the Hellespont into Asia Minor (modern Turkey) in 334. An ensuing victory in the Battle of Granicus secured Ionia, and the following year he defeated Darius III's forces at the Battle of Issus in southern Asia Minor, opening the western half of the Persian Empire to him. Except for Tyre, the Phoenician cities along the eastern shore of the Mediterranean quickly capitulated. Needing supplies, he ordered Jerusalem and neighboring cities to furnish men, war materiel, and tribute, in the amount ordinarily given to Darius. Tyre acquiesced after a seven-month siege, and Alexander then continued down the Mediterranean coast toward Palestine. The first-century historian Flavius Josephus claims that Alexander met the high priest Jaddua on the road to Jerusalem and made obeisance after recognizing him as the figure he had seen in a dream urging him to take the Persian Empire. Proceeding to Jerusalem, which offered no resistance, supposedly he sacrificed in the temple and granted privileges to the Jews. The contemporary scholar Elias Bickerman questions the Josephus account, however, claiming that since Syrian and Samarian cities had capitulated, it seems doubtful that Judeans would resist, in view of Alexander's superior force. In all likelihood, Bickerman insists, it was Jaddua who submitted to Alexander, who then gave the Judeans permission to live according to their ancestral laws. Bickerman feels—whether rightly or wrongly is uncertain—the entire story of Alexander's visit to Jerusalem

---

1. Lerner et al., *Western Civilizations*, 132–35.

is "probably fictitious, invented to flatter Jewish self-esteem."² Regardless of what really occurred, Judea did not resist the invader, and the Jews' status continued as it had been under the Persians; they continued paying tribute and practicing their religious rituals in the customary way, and the temple's function was unchanged.³

Alexander continued down the coast and took Egypt, which submitted peacefully. In 331, at the Battle of Gaugamela, near Irbil in today's northern Iraq, he delivered a final blow to Persia, bringing the wealth of Susa and Persepolis into his control. He then marched east into Bactria (Afghanistan) and on to the Indus River Valley in India, before turning back, when his army resisted going any farther. He returned to Babylon, where he died of fever in 323 at age thirty-two.

Following Alexander's sudden death, his generals initially tried to maintain the empire's unity. By 305, however, all hope of holding his domain together had ended, and fighting occurred among the competing generals. The empire finally divided after the decisive Battle of Ipsis (in Phyrgia) in 301, with Cassander holding Macedon, Seleucus getting Syria, and Ptolemy taking Egypt, including Palestine. By 280 three ruling dynasties descended from Alexander's generals had emerged: the Antigonid in Macedon, the Seleucid in Syria, and the Ptolemaic in Egypt.⁴ Palestine remained a bone of contention between the Seleucids and Ptolemies, and they fought repeatedly over it; these conflicts, however, had little internal impact on Palestine.

Judea remained a client province of Ptolemaic Egypt during the third century, which proved to be a time of stability. The Egyptian court kept no governor in Jerusalem, but royal troops garrisoned the city's fortress, and Jews furnished troops for the imperial army, including a Jewish cavalry regiment. In practice, Judea was a self-governing unit of Ptolemaic Egypt. Its ruling body, with administrative and judicial authority, was the Council of Elders led by the high priest, whom the king appointed for life. The high priest was responsible for raising the tribute, the annual lump-sum payment to the royal treasury. Ptolemaic taxation relied on tax farming; under this system the high priest distributed tax farming rights to local nobles, making him the intermediary between the crown and the Judeans—in

---

2. Bickerman, *Jews in the Greek Age*, 5.

3. Ferguson, *Backgrounds of Early Christianity*, 403; Bickerman, *Jews in the Greek Age*, 4–7; Josephus, *Ant.* 11.8.5.

4. Ferguson, *Backgrounds of Early Christianity*, 15–16, 403–04; Bickerman, *Jews in the Greek Age*, 22.

effect, the nation's head. The nobles received authority to collect taxes and keep a portion as payment for their services, giving the aristocracy an interest in supporting Ptolemaic domination.[5]

Palestine, as a province of Ptolemaic Egypt, seemingly was a desirable place to live, especially for upper-class Jews, if one can judge by the example of the influential Tobiad clan. As a young man, Joseph, one of its members, rose to prominence in the late third century. When the high priest Oniad failed to pay the tax allotment, Joseph went to Egypt and convinced the king to award him the tax concession. He amassed considerable wealth as a tax farmer, and became a well-known financier and businessman. He was frequently seen at the royal court, and became a spokesman for Jews.[6]

Jews also fared quite well in Ptolemaic Egypt. Some came from the Persian Empire, and the Ptolemies needed workers to develop the Nile valley's rich agricultural potential; Alexander had brought Jews from Samaria, and following his death, when his generals were vying for regional control, Ptolemy I (304-283) transferred more to Egypt during his campaigns in Palestine, some as the king's captives and others as his soldiers' slaves. They were settled at various garrisons, and in Alexandria, the delta city Alexander had founded, where they joined earlier Jewish settlers. Jews also migrated to Egypt independently, for they saw it as an attractive place to live. Ptolemy II (285-46) eventually freed the Jews who were serving in captivity. Alexandria became the major center of the Jewish dispersion, and Jews played a substantial role in Ptolemaic economic and political life.[7]

In the ongoing rivalry for regional control, the Seleucids eventually triumphed. Seleucid forces decisively defeated the Egyptians around 200 at Banyas in Palestine, near the source of the Jordan River, bringing Judea under Syrian control. The Judeans welcomed the Seleucids, in part because of their links to fellow Jews in Babylonia, which was also under Seleucid control. Initially the transition to Seleucid suzerainty made little difference in Judean life. Antiochus III (223-187), the Seleucid king, upheld Judean national customs and autonomous status by royal decree, and internal administration remained in the hands of the high priest and Council of Elders, and the temple complex retained its tax exemption.[8]

---

5. Bickerman, *From Ezra to the Last of the Maccabees*, 54-57.

6. Grant, *History of Ancient Israel*, 201-2; Josephus, *Ant.* 12.4.1-5.

7. Ferguson, *Backgrounds of Early Christianity*, 404; Bickerman, *Jews in the Greek Age*, 81-82; Josephus, *Ant.* 12.1.1.

8. Grant, *History of Ancient Israel*, 204-5; Bickerman, *Jews in the Greek Age*, 123-25.

Trouble eventually arose, however, because of changes stirring in the Mediterranean world, where Rome was rising to dominance. Having subdued the Italian peninsula by the mid-third century, Rome defeated Carthage, a rival power across the Mediterranean in present-day Tunisia, after a century-long struggle—the Punic Wars—the second phase of which ended in 202. Rome then turned its attention to the east, to punish Philip V of Macedon for aiding Carthage. This led to early-second-century hostilities with the eastern Mediterranean monarchies that arose after the division of Alexander's short-lived empire. The Romans won a series of victories over the Syrian monarch Antiochus III, culminating in their decisive triumph at Magnesia in Asia Minor in 190. This deprived the Syrians of their eastern Mediterranean holdings, and the Romans extracted such a heavy tribute that the Syrians thereafter experienced heavy financial pressure. To help pay the Roman levy, Seleucus IV (187–75), Antiochus's successor, imposed heavy taxes on his subjects. The land tax, for example, to which Judeans were subject, rose to nearly one-third the value of the crop raised on it.[9]

Thus, in the era following the Israelites' return from Babylon, as the power base in the eastern Mediterranean and the Middle East shifted, they were successively subject to several sovereign regimes—the Persians, then Alexander, and when his short-lived empire divided, to the Ptolemies, until they were replaced by the Seleucids. For the most part, they enjoyed a good measure of autonomy under these foreign entities. But Rome's advance into the eastern Mediterranean in the second century BCE resonated in Judea. The financially stressed Seleucids compensated for Rome's heavy tribute with excessive taxation of their Judean clients. The oppressive burden of Syrian taxation, however, wasn't the only force impinging on second-century Judean life, for with Alexander the Great came more than military victory. His remarkable but short-lived empire's permanent legacy was the spread of Greek-like culture throughout the Middle East. Inevitably this impacted Palestine.

---

9. Ferguson, *Backgrounds of Early Christianity*, 405–06.

III

Jews Meet Greeks

"Hellenism" is the usual term scholars use when referring to Greek-like culture. Hellenism was present in the Middle East to a limited degree prior to Alexander's late-fourth-century invasion, but as he advanced east he took steps to consolidate his control; these accelerated its spread. For example, he replaced Persian with Greek governors. Some seventy cities were founded as outposts of Greek domination, and retired soldiers and Greek immigrants were settled in them to keep the conquered people subdued. In Palestine, Samaria was transformed into a military colony by removing many city residents to Shechem, about twenty miles north of Jerusalem, and replacing them with Greek settlers, who were encouraged to intermarry with local people. These measures intensified Hellenism's regional penetration, opening the door for it to impact Second Temple Jewish life. To gain insight into how this occurred, however, it is essential to learn what constituted some of Hellenism's main features and see where Judean and Hellenistic culture intersected.

Following the breakup of Alexander's empire in the early third century, the Seleucids continued promoting Hellenism, helping to fix its impact on the region. They built many new cities and reorganized others in the Greek manner with municipal self-governments, tribal-based citizen councils, primary assemblies of citizens, responsible magistrates, and their own laws and finances. Judea was virtually surrounded with hellenized towns: Ascalon, Ptolemais, Joppa, and Apollonia on the coast; Samaria, Scythopolis, and Gadara in the north; Pella, Gerasa, and Philadelphia (Rabbath Amana) across the Jordan; and Marisa in the south.[1]

Judeans now came into direct contact with Greeks more frequently. There were many Greek officers, civil agents, and traders, and Greek caravans visited Jerusalem. Extant papyri record Greek residents in Judea trading in slaves, wine, oil, honey, figs, and dates, and loaning money. To facilitate these commercial transactions, there must have been people in Judean villages capable of preparing contracts in Greek.[2] As Greek increasingly became the language of commerce and government, aristocratic Jews, anxious to improve their socioeconomic status, would have included Greek in their children's education.[3] Jews were introduced to Greek culture as upper-class children learned Greek, Greek officials and traders became more numerous in Judea, and settlers in neighboring hellenized towns replicated the life they had left in their homeland.

This new culture contained features that contrasted starkly with the Judeans' Torah-based traditions. According to the fifth-century poet Simonides, the dominant aspirations of Greek life were "to be in health," the "best thing"; "the next best, to be of form and nature beautiful; the third, to enjoy wealth gotten without fraud; and the fourth, to be in youth's bloom among friends."[4] Will Durant, the twentieth-century historian, reduced them to the "worship of health, beauty, and strength."[5]

Greeks celebrated these values in their great festivals dominated by athletics, the oldest and greatest of which was the Olympiad that occurred every four years at Olympia, sanctuary of the Greeks' chief god Zeus, ruler of gods and men. The city-state Utica's method of preparing competitors for the games reveals the importance Greeks attached to the Olympiad. Its twenty-four best athletes were selected through local, municipal, and city-state competitions. These winners then trained for ten months under professional coaches. On arriving at Olympia for the games, all participants were registered, examined for physical defects, and sworn to uphold the festival's rules. Identified by city-state, they marched in nude procession

---

1. Ferguson, *Backgrounds of Early Christianity*, 19, 403; Bickerman, *From Ezra to the Last of the Maccabees*, 58,; Bickerman, *Jews in the Greek Age*, 124; Grant, *History of Ancient Israel*, 199; Lerner et al., *Western Civilizations*, 133, 137.

2. Bickerman, *From Ezra to the Last of the Maccabees*, 59.

3. Ferguson, *Backgrounds of Early Christianity*, 403.

4. Simonides, in Durant, *Life of Greece*, 211.

5. Durant, *Life of Greece*, 211.

into the stadium before its forty-five thousand spectators. Sacrifices to Zeus were periodically offered as the athletes competed in the pentathlon, the five most important sports: the broad jump, discus throw, javelin throw, stadium sprint (two hundred yards), and wrestling. All participants competed in each event, and the winner had to be tops in three. Horse and chariot racing were added, competitions requiring a hippodrome to be built near the stadium. At the games' close, winners received a wild olive garland as a herald announced their names and city-states. On arriving home, they were feted lavishly and awarded substantial sums.

In time other festivals similar to the Olympiad appeared elsewhere in Greece. Delphi sponsored the Pythian Games in honor of Apollo, the god of prophecy, and Corinth founded the Isthmian Games, to honor Poseidon, god of the sea and brother of Zeus. As the number of festivals grew, the competitions expanded to include the arts: poetry, oratory, recitations, drama, dance, painting, and sculpture, as well as vocal and instrumental music. A combination of athletic and artistic competitions and fairs, the festivals were panhellenic events of great importance. They were heroic ecumenical occasions, steeped in civic pride, during which all other activities, even war, ceased. The winners stood at the apex of Greek celebrity.[6]

Undoubtedly some young Judeans dreamed of gaining celebrity by participating in the Greek festivals. For others, especially those of upper-class standing, skill in the Greek language brought the prospect of access to the financial and administrative world. Facility in Greek, however, also yielded another significant, if unanticipated, benefit; it opened the door to Greek intellectual life, where seminal developments were occurring.[7]

From the sixth to the fourth century Greek thinkers were asking probing questions about the nature of the universe and the meaning of life. While their Babylonian counterparts were attributing events in the physical order to occult forces moving the stars, the skeptical Greeks rejected such supernatural causes and sought rational—rather than supernatural—explanations for the material world. They were the first people in the ancient world to do so, and in the process laid the foundation for the discipline of philosophy.

Some sixth-century Greek intellectuals speculated that all things were formed from some primary substance, but disagreed on what it was. Thales believed it was water. A century later Democritus called the primary substance "atoms"—minute indestructible particles existing in almost infinite

---

6. On the festivals, see Durant, *Life of Greece*, 211–17.
7. Ferguson, *Backgrounds of Early Christianity*, 403.

number—and theorized that all material objects consist of atoms in chance combination. These efforts to look for natural laws, and rational, rather than supernatural explanations to account for the physical world, were new.[8]

Pythagoras taught that the essence of things was found beyond the material realm, in the study of numbers. Geometry students still learn his famous theorem: the square on the hypotenuse of a right-angled triangle equals the sum of the squares on the other two sides. In avoiding the material world in his search for meaning and truth, he nevertheless remained characteristically Greek—rational—in looking for laws and regularities in the abstract world of numbers.[9]

Differing schools of thought about the great questions that the new thinkers (philosophers) were asking emerged in fifth-century Greece. The Sophists—"those who are wise," or "those who know things"—followed Pythagoras's teaching, that "man is the measure of all things." This meant that concepts like truth, goodness, and justice were conventions rooted in human interests and needs. The only avenue to knowledge, he claimed, was through sensory perception, which meant that each individual perceived the world through his own senses and constructed his own version of valid truths, ruling out the possibility of transcendent truth. Sophists claimed the wise person would question all traditions and objectively examine each situation to determine which course of action was best.[10]

Critics believed that Sophism was socially dangerous. If goodness and justice were merely the product of individual preference, consensus on acceptable behavior would be impossible. Society could not be sustained and anarchy would prevail. This fear induced the rise of a school of thought asserting the existence of absolute standards. Socrates, a fifth-century Athenian patriot who cared deeply for the city, worried that Sophism would destroy it. The search for truth, he advocated, must begin by carefully defining terms, and continue by subjecting all inherited assumptions to reexamination. He anchored his system of truth in ethics—how individuals act toward others. He advocated continually assessing personal conduct for one's own, and society's, good, for, as he said, "the unexamined life is not worth living." Socrates idled in the Athenian marketplace, posing questions to those eager for discussion. Needing a scapegoat to account for the city's defeat in the Peloponnesian War, Athenians eventually blamed his constant

8. Lerner et al., *Western Civilizations*, 106, 140.
9. Lerner et al., *Western Civilizations*, 106.
10. Lerner et al., *Western Civilizations*, 107.

questioning of tradition for undermining the integrity of Athens's youth and condemned him to death. The essential difference between Socrates and the Sophists was that he believed a standard of absolute truth existed, which the Sophists denied. Their ethics rested on expediency—whatever worked. Sophists were pragmatists.[11]

Plato (429-349) combined Socrates's ideas into a coherent philosophical system. To refute the Sophists' dangerous skepticism, he sought a secure foundation for his ethics in his doctrine of ideas. He acknowledged the material world's reality, but believed the physical order was only one aspect of the universe. There was also a higher abstract or spiritual realm, consisting of eternal forms he called "ideas." Each of these was the pattern of some class of objects that exist on earth—the idea of chair, shape, color, beauty, justice, etc. The greatest of these was the idea of good, which he believed was the cause and guiding purpose of the universe. What humans perceive through their senses are only imperfect copies of these supreme realities, much like the relation of shadows to real objects. The realm of ideas is true and eternal, while earthly life is temporary and corruptible. The good life, he said, should seek to enter as fully as possible into the realm of ideas. Since that realm is abstract and spiritual, it can be entered only by subduing one's physical side and cultivating intellectual or spiritual qualities. (Plato uses the terms "intellectual" and "spiritual" interchangeably). Guided by this outlook on earth, the soul will be prepared for union with good in the afterlife.[12] (Plato's idea of "the good" vaguely resembles the Judeo-Christian concept of an omnipotent God. However, he doesn't talk about God, and never advocated any system of divine worship. And there is little chance that Plato was influenced by Jewish prophets, although some Christians wondered about that possibility).

Plato's student Aristotle (384-22) was more practically oriented. He acknowledged the reality of material objects and believed that by systematic study of how they functioned one could understand nature and nature's plan. His central conclusion was that all things in the universe consist of the imprint of form on matter. In other words, the universe was teleological (had purpose) and nature's function was to shape matter. As for ethics, Aristotle sought never to "have his head in the clouds." He focused on life in this world in the present rather than as a path to otherworldly salvation. The highest good for humans was self-realization, the harmonious functioning

---

11. Lerner et al., *Western Civilizations*, 108-09.
12. Lerner et al., *Western Civilizations*, 109-10.

of mind and body. They find happiness by exercising their rational ability appropriately—applying reason to practical matters. To Aristotle, virtuous conduct meant striving for balance in all activity—the "golden mean"—rather than rashness or cowardice, moderation rather than indulgence or excessive self-denial.[13]

Aristotle identified "nature" as the presiding force in the universe. By imposing order on the physical material that makes up the universe, rather than leaving matter to randomly clash with itself, nature was a benevolent force. Plato, on the other hand, relied on the vague notion of "good" as the cause and guiding force in the universe. Neither, however, accounted for the origin of nature or good. This stands in stark contrast to the Jewish worldview, whose point of departure was the origin of nature and good. On life's great questions, Jews relied on revelation, while Greeks asked questions and resorted to reason.

As Greek culture became more pervasive in Judean life in the fourth and third centuries, Greek philosophers continued generating new understandings about the nature of the universe and the meaning of life. This expanded the world of ideas open to consideration by curious Jews as growing numbers of them learned Greek. The two most prominent schools of thought in the Hellenistic world were Stoicism and Epicureanism. They shared certain ideas. Both were individualistic, allotting centrality to the individual rather than society. They were materialistic, denying the existence of any spiritual quality in the universe. The two outlooks also contained an element of universalism, believing that all human beings were the same the world over. Otherwise, they arrived at very different conclusions about the nature of the cosmos.

Zeno, an Athenian who lived around 300, fathered Stoicism. He held that the cosmos was an orderly whole, where all evident contradictions are ultimately resolved. Evil, by which he meant the misfortunes that afflict humans, is only a series of necessary events on the way to the final perfection of the universe. All that happens is rigidly determined in accordance with rational purpose. Individuals are not master of their own fate, but merely links in an unbroken chain of events. People are free to rebel or accept their fate, but they cannot change or overcome it. The individual's supreme duty is to submit to fate (the order of the universe) in the belief that that order is ultimately good, even though one doesn't perceive it to be so. The truly happy person submits to the order that fate imposes on him, and

---

13. Lerner et al., *Western Civilizations*, 111.

purges himself of bitterness. By resignation to fate, one achieves the highest happiness—serenity or peace of mind. The Stoics' ethics emphasized self-control and forgiveness of one another. The virtuous person exhibited these characteristics.[14]

Epicureanism took its name from Epicurus, another Athenian whose life spanned the late fourth and early third centuries. The Epicurean point of departure was the atomism of Democritus, who, it will be recalled, believed that when atoms—minute indestructible particles existing in almost infinite number—combine randomly, they produce all physical objects. This being the case, there was no ultimate purpose in the universe, which functions by itself, without supernatural intervention. Epicureans held that the highest good is pleasure, not the pleasure of abandonment to hedonism in endless carousing (as is often mistakenly believed), but the satisfaction of contemplating excellence and experiencing peacefulness. Serenity of soul, they claimed, comes from eliminating fear, especially fear of the supernatural, the source of the greatest mental pain. As materialists, Epicureans believed that the soul was material and did not outlast the body, which eliminated fear of an afterlife. They rejected the existence of absolute justice, but held that duly considered laws are beneficial and should be obeyed for the common good. They had no hope of eliminating evil through human effort, so a thinking person would withdraw from undertaking social obligation and be content with studying philosophy and enjoying friends.[15]

While Alexander's empire proved to be short-lived, its lasting contribution was to imprint Greek-like culture permanently on the Middle East, a development that inevitably reverberated in Judea. As Judeans increasingly crossed paths with Greeks and growing numbers learned the Greek language, they encountered a plethora of understandings about the nature of the physical world and the meaning of life. Schooled in the traditions of the law and the temple, Judeans found much in Hellenism that clashed with the teachings of the Torah, and their response was mixed.

Conservative Jews, the Hasidim ("righteous ones"), zealous for the law's sanctity, opposed the drift to Greek ways, believing that all Greek influence should be "resisted root and branch."[16] The second-century Book of Jubilees lamented Judea's moral skid during a century and a half of close contact with Greeks, for an evil generation had arisen that ignored the commandments

---

14. Lerner et al., *Western Civilizations*, 138–39.
15. Lerner et al., *Western Civilizations*, 139–40.
16. Grant, *History of Ancient Israel*, 205.

and the Sabbath. Parents were refusing to circumcise their sons; the author invoked the traditional Jewish prohibition against appearing naked in order to discourage young Jews from participating in Greek games, where athletes competed nude.[17] Eager to counteract Greek influence, Ben Sira, the contemporary author of Ecclesiasticus, or the Wisdom of Jesus Son of Sirach, denounces Jews "ashamed of the Torah," and "ungodly men who have forsaken the Law of the Most High God."[18] The Book of Maccabees tells of Jews scandalized at seeing "young aristocrats in Jerusalem wearing broad-brimmed Greek hats" and "young priests hastening to finish their duties at the temple" in order to go and "exercise naked in the Greek manner at the gymnasium." More deplorable was learning that some youths had undergone surgery to "hide their circumcision" to avoid ridicule by Greeks.[19]

On the other hand, "advanced" Jews, as they were called, saw Hellenism as a new, technologically superior influence that was progressive and up to date.[20] It was the locus of the world's mighty leaders, as Alexander's success made abundantly clear. There were upper-class Jews who were "convinced that a certain infusion of Greek ways had proved unavoidable, and indeed desirable, if their people was not to fall behind the modern cosmopolitan world."[21] To curious young Judean aristocrats proficient in Greek, the philosophers' grand speculations, which cast doubt on supernatural explanations about the nature of the material world and provided alternate insights about life's meaning, offered an alluring body of new thought for their consideration. By the third and second centuries BCE Greek culture clearly had begun to compete with Jewish tradition rooted in the Torah, and was becoming a divisive force in Judea.

---

17. Bickerman, *From Ezra to the Last of the Maccabees*, 59–60.

18. Bickerman, *From Ezra to the Last of the Maccabees*, 60.

19. 1 Macc 1:13–15, and 2 Macc 4:10–17, cited in Ferguson, *Backgrounds of Early Christianity*, 405.

20. Bickerman, *From Ezra to the Last of the Maccabees*, 59.

21. Grant, *History of Ancient Israel*, 205.

IV

Antiochus Epiphanes, the Abomination of Desolation, and the Maccabean Rebellion

HAVING COMPLETED THIS EXCURSION into the world of Hellenism, and its growing impact in Judea, it is necessary to return to the narrative of events in Jerusalem in the mid-second century. The contrasting reactions to the presence of Greek influence brought friction in Judean society, as hellenizers and conservative Jews competed for control. This cleavage became entangled with the Seleucid monarchy's policies, and grew into a violent struggle during the reign of Antiochus IV Epiphanes (175–63), with enduring consequences.

Trouble arose shortly after Antiochus came to power, when the interests of the rival Oniad and Tobiad families in Judea clashed. The Oniads had held the high priestly office since the days of Zadok in David's reign, while the Tobiads exercised the right to collect taxes under the Ptolemies and seemingly also under the Seleucids. In 174 the Tobiads raised allegations of scandal against Oniad high priest Onias III, who went to Antioch, the Seleucid capitol in Syria, to defend himself. The outcome was that Onias's brother Jason, seemingly with a substantial Tobiad bribe, was appointed high priest, while Onias was assassinated. In Jerusalem the hellenizers sought to exploit the friction-filled atmosphere to advance their political objectives. Jason, now high priest, hoped to oblige them by quickening the pace of hellenization in the city. He reorganized Jerusalem's government in keeping with Greek practice, changing it from a temple-city to a Greek city-state, with a council and citizen list. A gymnasium, the traditional focal point of Greek life, was built, as well as an ephebum, a building or court, where young, uncircumcised males (*ephebes*) exercised nude, in keeping with Greek custom.[1]

However, the Hellenizing Jews, anxious for power, were not content with Jason's modest reforms. Led by the Tobiads, they now supported Menelaus, who belonged to a second-grade priestly house, as high priest. After outbidding Jason, presumably with Tobiad aid, Menelaus was awarded the office in 172, thereby breaking the traditional Zadokite high priestly line. This offended the law-conscious traditionalist Jews and intensified their clash with the hellenizers.[2]

Meanwhile Antiochus, hoping to extend his rule to Egypt, needed funds. Menelaus accommodated him, and together they plundered the temple treasury in 169, enabling Antiochus's Egyptian project to proceed. It was on the verge of succeeding when Rome, the rising power in the Mediterranean, forced him to withdraw. Rumor spread in Jerusalem that Antiochus had died in Egypt, and Jason, intent on retrieving his office, hastily moved against Menelaus. When he learned that Antiochus actually was still alive, however, Jason abandoned Jerusalem rather than risk facing Antiochus's vengeance. Intending to inflict punishment for Jason's revolt, Antiochus moved with force against Jerusalem. He demolished the city's wall, and then built a new citadel—the Acra—adjacent to the temple and garrisoned it with Syrian forces to dominate the temple area, where hellenizers had flocked for protection.[3]

After reclaiming the office of high priest, Menelaus and the hellenizers, with garrison support, boldly converted temple ritual into worship of a Semitic god, the Lord of Heaven, who was identified with the Greek god Zeus. Then in 167 Antiochus issued decrees—subsequently known in Jewish history as the Abomination of Desolation—virtually obliterating customary Jewish religious observances; the Scriptures were to be destroyed, Sabbath

1. Ferguson, *Backgrounds of Early Christianity*, 405; Grant, *History of Ancient Israel*, 208.

2. Ferguson, *Backgrounds of Early Christianity*, 405–6; Grant, *History of Ancient Israel*, 207–08.

3. Ferguson, *Backgrounds of Early Christianity*, 405–6; Grant, *History of Ancient Israel*, 207–08.

Antiochus Epiphanes, the Abomination of Desolation, and the Maccabean Rebellion

observance and festivals abandoned, food laws abolished, and circumcision prohibited. In the temple a second altar was built over the great altar of burnt offering, and, in a supreme insult to Jewish religion, pigs—animals Jews considered ritually unclean—were offered on it during the Feast of Dionysus. Throughout Jerusalem those wishing to display zeal for the new pagan cult built altars for sacrifice at their doors. Many complied with the decrees, while others resorted to evasion without appearing defiant, for openly avoiding the rite risked seizure and death. Some fled the city.[4]

There is uncertainty about why Antiochus implemented such decrees, so abominable to Jews. Many see them as evidence of Antiochus's intentional persecution of Jewish religion. On the other hand, perhaps mandating religious uniformity throughout his domain in order to strengthen Syria in view of the ongoing Parthian threat explains Antiochus's resort to the decrees. Others hold that the initiative for the decrees came from the extreme hellenizers, who believed that the only way to achieve their goal was to win Antiochus's support by eliminating traditional Judean religious practices.[5]

Whatever the true explanation, when Antiochus sent agents into the countryside, where Hellenism had been slower to penetrate, to enforce compliance with his decrees, they encountered resistance. This rural opposition was bolstered by those who had fled Jerusalem. Antiochus's officers erected altars in town marketplaces and summoned the populace to participate in pagan worship by eating the flesh of the sacrifice. Some complied, but others refused and were killed. In the Judean town of Modin a short distance northwest of Jerusalem, the officers called on a local figure named Mattathias to participate in the worship as an example to the townspeople. As a priest who had fled from Jerusalem to avoid being forced to practice the worship there, he refused. When another townsman volunteered to take his place, Mattathias killed him, and one of the king's agents. After destroying the altar, Mattathias and his sons fled into the surrounding hill country, where a sizable following of those eager to uphold the law, their cherished Torah, rallied round them.[6] Mattathias's family, the Hasmoneans (known

---

4. Ferguson, *Backgrounds of Early Christianity*, 406–7; Bickerman, *From Ezra to the Last of the Maccabees*, 93–96.

5. Ferguson, *Backgrounds of Early Christianity*, 407. Elias Bickerman claims that the high priest Jason convinced Antiochus to introduce "new customs contrary to the Torah" because the reformers wanted to assimilate. See Bickerman, *Jews in the Greek Age*, 129.

6. Ferguson, *Backgrounds of Early Christianity*, 407; Bickerman, *From Ezra to the Last of the Maccabees*, 96.

in Jewish history as the Maccabees—"the hammerers"), then organized a resistance movement which soon developed into a full-blown rebellion.

In 166 or 165, shortly before his death, Mattathias assigned the movement's leadership to Judas, one of his five sons; he proved to be a skilled military tactician and leader. From wilderness hideaways he led a guerilla campaign against the Syrians and their Hellenizing supporters, raiding villages and destroying the pagan altars Antiochus's officers had erected. They killed Hellenistic sympathizers and even circumcised children by force. When Syrian forces wiped out a body of Jews who had refused to defend themselves on the Sabbath in violation of the law, the Hasidim ("righteous ones") withdrew their opposition to Sabbath fighting and threw their support to the Hasmonean rebels. Judas had continued success in the rebellion, for the Syrians were struggling to control a Parthian uprising along their eastern border and could not marshal their full forces against the rebelling Judeans.

In response to the forceful Hasmonean resistance Antiochus finally withdrew his odious decrees in 165 or 164, but he left Menelaus in the office of high priest and kept troops in the Acra. Judas now moved his forces into Jerusalem. Their presence kept the Syrian forces in the Acra occupied while the temple was cleansed. The pagan altar was discarded in an "unclean place" and the sacred furniture restored. The defiled altar of burnt offering was dismantled and its stones deposited "in a convenient place on the temple hill until there should come a prophet to tell what to do with them."[7] Then a new altar was built, according to the law's specifications. The temple was rededicated and the traditional sacrifice of the burnt offering reinstated. (To commemorate this important event a new festival—the Festival of Lights, Hanukkah—was commissioned, and is still celebrated by Jews today.)

As these events unfolded in Jerusalem, Antiochus was in the east attempting to subdue the rebellious Parthians. Before leaving Antioch, he had appointed Lysias to act as regent in his absence, and charged him to watch over his nine-year-old son, the heir to the imperial throne. Antiochus died in Persia in 163, evidently the victim of the crushing weight of the mounting problems he faced; the Parthian campaign was failing, his funds were rapidly dwindling, military reinforcements he expected from Antioch never arrived, and word came that Lysias had failed to quell the Judean rebellion. This undoubtedly caused Antiochus to lose faith in him, and likely

---

7. Ferguson, *Backgrounds of Early Christianity*, 408.

Antiochus Epiphanes, the Abomination of Desolation, and the Maccabean Rebellion

explains why, shortly before dying, he appointed his friend Philip imperial regent, with authority to make his young son Antiochus king. When news of Antiochus's death reached Antioch, Lysias, anticipating a struggle over the imperial succession, quickly enthroned the nine-year-old boy as Emperor Antiochus V Eupator.[8]

Foreseeing an inevitable contest between Lysias and Philip to guide the youthful emperor, Judas Maccabaeus saw a promising opportunity to advance Judean autonomy. He believed Lysias would hesitate to leave Antioch lest Philip return with his army, while Philip would likely resist abandoning the campaign against the Parthians to return to Antioch. However, Judas misjudged Lysias, for when he attacked the citadel to drive out the Syrians, Lysias led an army south to rescue the besieged garrison. But as Jerusalem was about to fall, word came that Philip's army was returning from the east, and Lysias withdrew his forces.

Before leaving, however, he negotiated a face-saving compromise with Jerusalem's leaders. It confirmed the Jews' right to practice their traditional religion in return for pledging their continued loyalty to Syria. Syrian troops would remain in the citadel, and the wall the Maccabees had built around the temple would be dismantled. Seemingly blaming High Priest Menelaus for Antioch's decrees, Lysias executed him, and sped back to Antioch to face Philip and his army.

The Judeans had retained the right to practice their religion and accustomed way of life, which the Syrians had threatened. This secured the objective the Hasidim had been pursuing since Antiochus first issued the offensive decrees, and they withdrew their support of the rebels. Judas and his supporters, however, were not satisfied, for they feared the Syrians might renew their religious oppression and continue promoting hellenization. Independence now became their goal, an objective that seemed within their grasp, given the problems besetting the Syrians, not the least of which was the developing struggle over the imperial succession.

The rebels pressed their cause with varying intensity and success over the next two decades, aided by the mounting difficulties facing the Syrians. Following Antiochus IV's death repeated clashes occurred among claimants to the throne: five different figures occupied it during a two-decade span, and at one point there were two emperors. Continued unrest along their eastern border necessitated ongoing military campaigns to maintain Syrian authority there and to regain provinces that had broken away. This

---

8. Pearlman, *Maccabees*, 141–63.

prevented Syria from marshaling its full military might against the Judean uprising, to say nothing of the impact on its shrinking treasury. The Syrians were also under growing pressure in the north, as we have seen, from the expanding Romans, while to the south the Ptolemies were eager to reclaim Judea. Moreover, there was the possibility that the Romans, the Parthians, and the Egyptians might cooperate against Syria. These interconnected factors weakened Syria and increased the Maccabees' chances of success during the mid-second century BCE.

Although Lysias readily defeated Philip's forces after returning to Antioch, his hope of becoming the power behind the newly-crowned nine-year-old Antiochus V was disrupted by a new throne claimant. Demetrius, son of Seleucus IV Philopater (Syrian emperor 187–75), had been denied his legitimate claim to the emperorship when, following his father's death, his uncle seized the throne and became Emperor Antiochus IV Epiphanes. Demetrius now returned to Syria from Rome, where he had been living, to claim his inheritance.[9] On arriving in Antioch the army defected to him. His supporters executed Lysias and the young Antiochus V, and the people acclaimed him emperor.[10]

Demetrius appointed Alcimus high priest to fill the vacancy left following Menelaus's execution. Coming from Aaronic stock, Alcimus was acceptable to the Hasidim, and to the hellenizers because he had been close to them without being a radical hellenizer. His appointment offended the Maccabees, however, for they saw him as a Seleucid appointee, empowered by the Syrian soldiers garrisoned in Jerusalem.[11] When Alcimus peremptorily executed some sixty Hasidim early in his tenure, it stirred Judas and the rebels into renewed action. They harassed and killed hellenizers in the countryside, recruited new militia, and threatened Alcimus and his Hellenizing supporters in Jerusalem. When Demetrius sent a force to Jerusalem to reinforce Alcimus's authority, Judas ambushed it on the way, and the soldiers fled.[12]

---

9. The treaty of Apamea in 188 BCE ended a war in which Rome had defeated Syria at the Battle of Magnesia in Asia Minor in 190. Syria renounced claim to extensive areas, surrendered its fleet and war elephants, paid a heavy indemnity, and gave Rome twenty selected hostages, among whom was Demetrius, the emperor's son. See Pearlman, *Maccabees*, 18.

10. Pearlman, *Maccabees*, 183–92.

11. Pearlman, *Maccabees*, 192–93.

12. Pearlman, *Maccabees*, 193–97.

Antiochus Epiphanes, the Abomination of Desolation, and the Maccabean Rebellion

While Judas was a skilled tactician, as a shrewd leader he also took advantage of regional political realities. Anticipating Syria's future absorption, Rome had withheld recognition of Demetrius as Seleucid king. Assuming Rome would consider joint measures with Syria's enemies, Judas sent emissaries to Rome. The mission resulted in a Rome-Maccabean mutual assistance pact in 161.[13] Surprisingly, Demetrius, intent on consolidating his newly-won position, was not deterred by the threat of Roman-Maccabean collaboration. He sent his general Bacchides south with a large force that defeated the heavily outnumbered Maccabees at Elasa, and killed Judas in 160.[14]

Following this victory Bacchides remained in Jerusalem and strengthened Syria's regional defenses by building new area fortresses and refurbishing others. At the time of Lysias's withdrawal from Jerusalem, as we have seen, the Jews had pledged their loyalty to Syria in order to secure their traditional rights; now, to ensure their continued loyalty, Bacchides lodged hostages from among their sons under guard in the Acra. This gave Alcimus and his Hellenizing Jewish compatriots a free hand to administer Jerusalem and, with Bacchides's help, pursue the Maccabees.[15]

Judas's death and Bacchides's presence in Jerusalem made continuing the Maccabean rebellion pointless temporarily, yet the rebels were not resigned to ultimate failure. They appointed Jonathan, the youngest of Judas's four remaining brothers, their new head. Although less gifted as a military leader than Judas, Jonathan nevertheless eventually would adeptly exploit regional power struggles to advance the Maccabean cause. In the meantime, he led the rebel forces into Tekoa, the desert region south of Jerusalem and west of the Dead Sea, where they recovered from their losses, retained their military organization, and lived to fight another day. The region's numerous caves afforded ample cover and were close enough to Jerusalem to enable Jonathan's intelligence network to remain abreast of developments in the city and the surrounding towns.[16]

Diplomatic maneuvering and intrigue by regional monarchs in response to periodic disputes among contenders for the Syrian throne eventually played into Jonathan's patient hands and resulted in Maccabean fortunes improving in 152. Demetrius unwisely intervened in a power struggle in Cappadocia, an Asia Minor kingdom previously controlled by

13. Pearlman, *Maccabees*, 197–201.
14. Pearlman, *Maccabees*, 203–07.
15. Pearlman, *Maccabees*, 207–09.
16. Pearlman, *Maccabees*, 209–11.

Syria, which awakened the hostility of kings in Cappadocia and neighboring Pergamum. His unsuccessful attempt to annex Cyprus, an Egyptian dependency, also aroused Ptolemy IV. In view of their common opposition to Demetrius the three kings backed Balas, an opportunist who fraudulently claimed to be Antiochus IV's son and the rightful heir to the Syrian throne. When Rome recognized Balas as the legitimate Syrian king, the three kings supported him, and, when he landed at Ptolemais and proclaimed himself king, the populace supported him.[17]

Isolated and facing war with Balas, and perhaps even Rome, Demetrius sought Maccabean support with a cordial appeal to Jonathan. He conferred the title of "King's Ally" on him with the right to raise an army, abandoned Syrian fortresses around Jerusalem, and released the hostages from the Acra. Jonathan responded by moving to Jerusalem, returning the released hostages to their families, and refortifying the temple precinct. In practice, this brought all Judea except Ptolemais and the Beth Zur fortress, which Demetrius maintained as a refuge for hellenized Jews, under Maccabean control.[18]

Balas attempted to outbid Demetrius for Jonathan's support. In an affable communication, accompanied by a crown and purple robe—the symbols of royal office—he appointed Jonathan high priest, with title "King's Friend." This step, which filled the office of high priest vacant for seven years following Alcimus's death, was welcomed in Jerusalem and treated as formal recognition of Jonathan's administrative and military leadership.[19]

With the struggle for the Syrian crown between Balas and Demetrius continuing, Demetrius repeated his appeal to Jonathan for support. However, in view of Demetrius's precarious position and the lingering Syrian-Judean hostility, Jonathan dismissed his overture as an act of desperation. He sided with Balas, who defeated Demetrius in 150 and gained the Syrian throne.[20]

This opened a period of cordial relations between the Seleucid monarchy and the Maccabees. Jonathan attended the marriage of Balas's daughter to Ptolemy, the Egyptian king. Balas made Jonathan a member of the "Order of King's Friends" and appointed him governor and commander in the king's service in Judea in 150. In effect, the Jews attained home rule; it

17. Pearlman, *Maccabees*, 219–20.
18. Pearlman, *Maccabees*, 220–24.
19. Pearlman, *Maccabees*, 224–25.
20. Pearlman, *Maccabees*, 226–29.

wasn't full independence, but, except for the presence of royal troops in the Acra, Jonathan was able to govern Judea freely without Balas interfering. The Maccabean nationalists became the ruling power in Judea, now a Jewish state in all but name. Jonathan maintained good relations with Balas for three years, and Judea was peaceful from 150 to 147.[21]

Strife over the Syrian throne reemerged in 147, however, when Demetrius's young son (also named Demetrius) landed in Cilicia with Cretan mercenaries, intent on claiming his dead father's throne. Balas, who opted to live at Ptolemais rather Antioch, had unwisely left administrative matters to officials in the Syrian capital, opening the way for his opponents to conspire against him. Friction was also mounting between Balas and Ptolemy, his Egyptian father-in-law, who had hoped unsuccessfully to gain influence in his son-in-law's Syrian kingdom that Egypt once ruled and wanted to reclaim. When Balas hurried north to check the invading young Demetrius, his grip on the Syrian crown was doubly threatened. Jonathan, with his brother Simon, came to Balas's aid, and together they defeated Demetrius's invading force. Balas rewarded Jonathan with membership in the royal order of "King's Kinsmen," and the gift of Ekron, a city on Palestine's coastal plain.[22]

Ptolemy now turned against Balas, and when he marched north to support Demetrius Balas fled to Cilicia. Ptolemy entered Antioch amid acclamation and briefly assumed the crown, making him monarch of both Egypt and the Seleucid Empire. However, knowing this would arouse Roman hostility, he wisely convinced the populace to accept Demetrius, who now became King Demetrius II Nicator. (Ptolemy probably believed that he would now achieve his goal of influencing Syrian affairs in view of Demetrius's gratitude, youth, and weakness.) Balas gathered fresh troops in Cilicia and reentered northern Syria, but Demetrius and Ptolemy's forces defeated him in a battle in which Ptolemy was seriously wounded. Balas fled to an Arab tribe that killed him. Ptolemy died shortly, and his forces withdrew from the coastal Palestinian areas they had occupied.[23]

Jonathan now only had to deal with the young and inexperienced Demetrius II who, while personally acceptable to the Syrians, was supported by his unpopular Cretan mercenaries. Determined to remove the last vestige of Syrian power in Judea, Jonathan laid siege to the Acra, still garrisoned by

21. Pearlman, *Maccabees*, 227–30.
22. Pearlman, *Maccabees*, 230–32.
23. Pearlman, *Maccabees*, 234–35.

Syrians. Demetrius ordered the siege raised and summoned Jonathan to a meeting. Jonathan defiantly maintained the siege, but attended the meeting which, surprisingly, proved to be a triumph for him, for he won Demetrius's confidence. He confirmed Jonathan's position as high priest and made him a first-class member of the "King's Friends." Three Samaritan districts were transferred to Judea, which was freed from tributes, tithes, and salt and crop taxes. These substantial concessions cost Jonathan only three hundred talents.[24] He returned to Jerusalem determined to consolidate his position in Judea, which had become a larger, stronger, and freer, though still not fully independent, entity.

Although Demetrius had succeeded in gaining the Syrian throne, he encountered domestic trouble when dissatisfaction among his troops spread to Antioch's citizenry. It grew into a popular uprising led by Diodotus, an officer who had deserted Balas to serve with Demetrius. Beseiged in his palace, Demetrius called for Jonathan's assistance. He sent troops on condition that Demetrius would remove his soldiers from the Acra. Jonathan's forces restored order in Antioch and Diodotus fled, but Demetrius reneged on his promise to evacuate the Acra garrison.[25]

More serious for Demetrius was the appearance of a new claimant for the Syrian throne in 144 or 143. Following Balas's death, his infant son had been entrusted to an Arab chieftain. The ambitious Diodotus (who took the name Tryphon) now presented the son as Antiochus VI, the rightful heir to the throne, with himself as regent. Backed by Demetrius's disaffected officers, Tryphon moved against Demetrius in the name of Antiochus VI. His forces triumphantly entered Antioch and Demetrius fled south to the coastal town of Seleucia. For a time Syria had two kings.

Again Jonathan was courted by the rival claimants to the Syrian throne. Because of his perfidious behavior, Demetrius could expect little support from Jonathan. Tryphon, eager to capitalize on Jonathan's growing power, enticed him in a friendly letter confirming his position as high priest and endorsing his authority in the three Samarian districts Demetrius had given him, and when Jonathan promised his support, Tryphon appointed Simon, Jonathan's brother, commander along Judea's Mediterranean coast. Abandoning hope of Jonathan's aid, Demetrius attacked him to secure southern Syria and Judea as a base from which to strike Tryphon.

---

24. Pearlman, *Maccabees*, 235.
25. Pearlman, *Maccabees*, 235.

However, Jonathan's forces defeated the army Demetrius sent south toward Galilee at Kedesh.[26]

With the struggle between Tryphon and Demetrius stalemated, Jonathan believed it timely to renew Judas's mutual assistance pact with Rome, and the senate received the mission he sent cordially. Jonathan doubtless had no illusions about Rome's real willingness to use force on Judea's behalf, but he likely believed that reconnecting with Rome formally would strengthen his hand. Demetrius, nevertheless, was determined to avenge his defeat at Kedesh, and sent an army south into Judea, which Jonathan's forces turned back without fighting when the northern invaders lost the element of surprise. Having checked Demetrius, Jonathan and Simon returned to Jerusalem. Expecting an eventual conflict with Tryphon, they convinced the elders to build defensive fortresses in Judea, strengthen Jerusalem's wall, and raise a barrier around the Acra to isolate its Syrian Garrison.[27]

Meanwhile Tryphon, anxious to consolidate his position, needed to ensure that Judea remained a Syrian province. This required eliminating Jonathan's growing power, and he sent an army south. Wary of Tryphon's intentions, Jonathan met him at Bethshean in northeastern Samaria. Unwilling to risk challenging Jonathan's surprisingly strong army, Tryphon reverted to deception. Feigning desire for cooperation, he greeted Jonathan with honors, and questioned why he was accompanied by an army when they were not at war. Jonathan, he deviously protested, should send his unneeded army home and accompany him to Ptolemais, which he intended to give him. With astonishing naivety, Jonathan dispatched most of his army to Jerusalem, and accompanied Tryphon to Ptolemais with a token force. Once inside the port city Tryphon sprang his trap; the gates were closed, Jonathan was seized, and his men were killed.[28]

Tryphon's treachery dejected the Judeans, for they assumed Jonathan had died with his men. With popular approval Simon assumed leadership of the Maccabees in 142, and he completed the improvements to Jerusalem's defenses which Jonathan had begun. When Tryphon advanced south from Ptolemais in force, Simon secured the strategic port of Jaffa and controlled the road from Jaffa to Jerusalem with his main force. The strength of Simon's force, however, surprised Tryphon. He sent word that Jonathan was alive and being held because of unpaid debt to the royal treasury; one

---

26. Pearlman, *Maccabees*, 236–38.
27. Pearlman, *Maccabees*, 238–41.
28. Pearlman, *Maccabees*, 243–45.

hundred silver talents and his two sons as hostages to guarantee he would not revolt in the future would secure his release. Suspecting deception, but fearing blame for Jonathan's probable death if he did not comply, Simon sent money and the children, but Jonathan wasn't freed.

While these negotiations were occurring, Tryphon continued marching south and entered Idumea, evidently intending to wheel north into Judea. Simon's army wisely shadowed these movements; a severe snowstorm combined with the superior strength of Simon's army persuaded Tryphon to abandon the invasion. He retreated up the Jordan Valley, but executed Jonathan before reaching Syria.[29] On reaching Antioch Tryphon removed the child king Antiochus VI and seized the throne. This intensified the struggle between himself and Demetrius II for the Seleucid Empire's crown.

Like Judas and Jonathan, Simon was eager for Judea's full independence. With Tryphon and Demetrius both looking to strengthen their political and military positions in preparation for a likely showdown, Simon believed the moment was right to approach Demetrius. He readily received Simon's emissaries and granted his demands; Judea was freed from all taxes, Demetrius renounced all claims for overdue tributes, and Simon's newly-built fortresses were left in Judean hands. These terms, which took effect immediately in 142, brought Judea virtual independence, and Simon became the first representative of the Hasmonean dynasty. The following year Syrian forces, and the hellenizers who had resided there, withdrew from the Acra, the last remaining symbol of Judea's tributary status.

Thus in 142 Judea was again an independent state. Somewhat larger than it had been as a Seleucid province, it spread west to the coastal plain, with territorial fringes extending marginally beyond the southern border (with Idumea) and the northern border (with Samaria) and into Transjordan in the east. Jaffa's harbor gave strategic access to the Mediterranean. Simon also captured Gazara (Gezer) and made it a strong military base under his son Johanan's (later known as Hyrcanus) command. Together with Adida, this protected Judea against attack from the coastal plain.[30]

Although Simon likely anticipated renewed military conflict with Tryphon and Demetrius, this did not occur. Having just failed to establish control over Judea, Tryphon evidently was not ready for a second attempt. Neither was Demetrius in a position to coerce Judea, for the Parthians had overrun the Province of Babylonia and the eastern portion of the Seleucid

---

29. Pearlman, *Maccabees*, 245–47.
30. Pearlman, *Maccabees*, 249–50.

Antiochus Epiphanes, the Abomination of Desolation, and the Maccabean Rebellion

Kingdom demanded his attention. The Seleucid Empire's continued division benefitted Judea as it asserted its independence. A great assembly met in Jerusalem in 140 and made Simon high priest and governor, with full responsibility for Judea's military security.

This was a significant step. It declared Judea's political independence by demonstrating that its source of authority was the will of the people rather than Syria. Its religious implication was revolutionary. Until Antiochus IV's time (175–64) the high priesthood was a hereditary office of the Oniads, whose roots went back to Zadok, David's high priestly appointee. After Onias II was deposed, high priests had been royal appointees, which offended traditionalist Jews, for some appointees were not from priestly families and the appointments were made by gentile rulers. Jonathan had been appointed by Balas. Clearly the high priestly appointment had to be regularized. There was no readily acceptable solution, however, for there were no longer any representatives of the House of Oniad, and no current prophet to authoritatively identify the divine will in the matter. The great assembly of 140, therefore, resorted to a provisional appointment, making the position a hereditary office of the Hasmoneans until a true prophet appeared with a permanent solution.[31]

With neither Tryphon nor Demetrius able to prevail in the struggle for control of Syria, Simon was able to consolidate his position. The temporary stability this brought lasted until 138, when a new claimant to the Syrian throne appeared. Demetrius had gone east to regain the dissident Province of Babylonia, leaving his wife Cleopatra in charge. However, the Parthian king Mithridates captured and held him for ten years. This induced Antiochus, Demetrius's younger brother then living in Rhodes, to return to Syria determined to restore the throne to the House of Seleucius. He proclaimed himself Emperor Antiochus VII (also known as Sidetes) and married Cleopatra. After gaining the confidence of Tryphon's enemies, he appealed to them and Simon for their support with promises of lavish rewards when he gained control of Syria. Tryphon fled to the vicinity of Caesarea on Judea's Mediterranean coast, which Antiochus then blockaded. Simon dispatched troops to aid him but, anticipating victory, Antiochus refused their help and repudiated his earlier promises. Overconfident, he demanded that Simon give up Jaffa, Gezer, and the Acra and threatened war if these demands were not met. When Simon rejected them, Antiochus sent a force into Judea, which Simon's son Hyrcanus defeated. Antiochus

---

31. Pearlman, *Maccabees*, 252–53.

made no further invasionary attempts, and Simon continued consolidating his position for the next three and a half years.[32]

While on an inspection tour near Jericho in 134, Simon was assassinated at a banquet given by his son-in-law Ptolemy, who evidently was secretly allied with Antiochus. (Seemingly Ptolemy hoped to gain the Judean governorship if Judea was restored to Syrian control.) Ptolemy then sent troops to capture Hyrcanus who, forewarned, intercepted them before returning to Jerusalem. Jerusalem's residents quickly recognized Hyrcanus as his father's successor and installed him as high priest, commander, and Judea's leader in 134.[33]

After four and a half centuries as a vassal of the Babylonians, the Persians, Alexander, the Ptolemies, and the Seleucids, Israel regained its independence. The Hasmoneans led the unlikely cause. Mattathias's bold defiance of Antiochus Epiphanes's decimation of Judea's religious rites with the Abomination of Desolation, in which the Hellenizing Jews were implicated, triggered the Maccabean uprising. On his father's death Judas assumed its leadership and guided the insurrection in the Judean countryside. Although Antiochus withdrew his offensive decrees, Judas was not appeased and transformed the insurrection into a nationalist rebellion whose goal was Judean independence. His death was a serious blow to the movement, but Jonathan wisely restrained the rebels until repeated conflicts among rival claimants to the Syrian throne weakened the Seleucid dynasty. This enabled him to choose which of the disputants to support in order to benefit the Maccabean cause, choices he exercised wisely. Independence finally came in 140 under Simon, the third Hasmonean brother.

---

32. Pearlman, *Maccabees*, 254–57.
33. Pearlman, *Maccabees*, 257.

V

The Hasmonean Kingdom

EARLY IN HYRCANUS'S TERM as high priest and Judean leader, his independence was seriously challenged, for with Tryphon's demise Antiochus VII threatened Judea. In 134 he invaded and laid siege to Jerusalem. With the city suffering a severe food shortage, however, a truce was arranged, for the Parthians were causing trouble for Antiochus. It required Judea to acknowledge its dependent status, pay a large indemnity, demolish Jerusalem's wall, and assist in Syria's Parthian war. In 130 Antiochus required Hyrcanus to accompany him on the Parthian campaign. Antiochus died in the ensuing fighting, and Demetrius II, a Parthian captive for the previous decade, as we have seen, returned to Syria and reclaimed the throne. He managed to hold it only briefly, and the Syrian kingdom thereafter disintegrated into individual principalities.[1]

Antiochus VII proved to be Syria's last strong ruler, and his passing enabled Hyrcanus to restore Judea's autonomy. He took advantage of the disorder in Syria accompanying Antiochus's brief tenure to consolidate his domestic position and then embarked on an expansionary foreign policy. Using mercenaries, he captured territory east of the Jordan River beyond the Dead Sea's northern tip, once part of David's kingdom. In Samaria he seized Shechem, occupied Mount Gerizim, and destroyed the Samaritan temple. On Judea's southern flank he forced the Idumeans to accept

1. Pearlman, *Maccabees*, 258.

circumcision and the Jewish law, thereby incorporating them into Jerusalem's religious community. Later his two sons, Aristobulus and Antigonus, captured Samaria's provincial capital. His policies seemingly offended the Pharisees, resulting in him gravitating to the Sadducees, whose Hellenistic proclivities were more attuned to his activities. He died in 104.[2]

Hyrcanus intended his wife to succeed him. However, Aristobulus, his eldest son, seized power, imprisoned three of his brothers and his mother, whom he starved to death when she challenged his assumption of power. He permitted his younger brother Antigonus to briefly share in governing until rumors against him arose among royal courtiers, and Aristobulus arranged his murder. He attacked the Itureans in northern Galilee and forced them to accept circumcision and Jerusalem's religious law, but his untimely death in 103 limited his rule to a single year. His wife, Salome Alexandra, released the three brothers from prison and named one of them, Jonathan, king and high priest, whom she then married. Her role during Jonathan's reign is uncertain, but it seems likely that she was quite influential, for she succeeded him after his death in 76.[3]

Reflecting his hellenization, Jonathan took the Greek name Alexander Jannaeus but was usually called Jannai. To secure his position, he murdered one of his two brothers but permitted the other, who eschewed political ambition, to live. He undercut the Council of Elders' authority by assuming the title of king, maintained a hellenized court and lived in a luxuriously secular manner. This, not to mention his personal degeneracy, incurred the enduring hostility of the Hasidim.[4]

Jannai was almost constantly at war, with varying degrees of success, and he soon faced opposition from his own subjects. Early in his reign he attacked the port of Ptolemais. Its residents appealed for help to Ptolemy Lathyrus, an Egyptian whose countrymen had banished him to Cyprus. Ptolemy's forces defeated Jannai at Asaphen on the middle Jordan River, but he escaped disaster when Egyptian opposition forced Ptolemy to withdraw. Free of Ptolemy, Jannai marched east of the Jordan and captured Gadara and Amathus, in the central lands east of the river; he then turned west to the coastal plain, took Raphia and Anthedon, and sacked Gaza. Later he subjugated the people of Moab and Gilead and advanced as far north as Gaulanitas beyond the Yarmuk River. This brought conflict with the Nabataeans, people

---

2. Noth, *History of Israel*, 386-87.
3. Noth, *History of Israel*, 387-88; Josephus, *Ant.* 13.11.1.
4. Noth, *History of Israel*, 388; Grant, *History of Ancient Israel*, 221-22.

southeast of the Dead Sea who also desired the land east of the Jordan; their forces ambushed him, but he escaped and fled to Jerusalem.

There he found that opposition to him was building, for many of Jerusalem's religious leaders resented his court's hellenization. They also opposed him being king as well as high priest, for they believed the royal title weakened the Council of Elders' authority. On one occasion, when Jannai appeared at the altar to offer sacrifice during the Feast of Tabernacles, the crowd pelted him with citrons. Then, in open rebellion with the Pharisees leading the way, they called on Seleucid leader Demetrius III, who controlled part of Syria around 90 BCE, for help in ridding them of Jannai. Near Shechem Demetrius's forces defeated Jannai, and he fled into the mountains. However, at Demetrius's moment of triumph, rather than see their monarch destroyed, the Judeans switched sides and came to Jannai's aid. Demetrius withdrew, and with the Judeans' help Jannai reasserted his authority and cruelly revenged himself on his enemies. Some eight hundred men were crucified, and as they died their wives and children were slaughtered before their eyes, while Jannai caroused with his courtesans. Thereafter he maintained his rule by terror that suppressed any further open domestic opposition. The Nabataeans continued their expansionist pressure east of the Jordan and remained Jannai's chief foreign threat to the end of his days.

Weakened by dissolute living, Jannai died prematurely in 76 while besieging Ragaba, a city east of the Jordan. He had inherited Judea, Samaria, and Galilee, and his conquests in the coastal plain secured the Mediterranean shoreline from the Egyptian border to Mount Carmel, and by taking territory in Transjordan he checked the menacing Nabataeans. His domain virtually equaled the ancient kingdoms of David and Solomon in extent, but he gained only limited domestic support and faced the enduring hostility of the Pharisees who despised his degenerate hellenized court. Mercenaries and extreme cruelty were required to maintain his power.[5]

On Jannai's death his ambitious wife, Alexandra Salome, seized power. Hyrcanus II, Jannai's oldest son, rightly should have had the throne. However, as he was indolent and irresolute, Salome made him high priest, and she struggled to restrain Aristobulus II, his aspiring younger brother. By expanding both the army and her mercenaries, she succeeded in preserving Hasmonean rule and avoiding war. Heeding Jannai's deathbed advice, she

---

5. Noth, *History of Israel*, 388-91; Ferguson, *Backgrounds of Early Christianity*, 410-11; Grant, *History of Ancient Israel*, 221-22.

established ties with the Pharisees, whom he had alienated, and reinstated their traditional practices which Hyrcanus I had abrogated. Accommodating the Pharisees' wishes, she welcomed the return of Jannai's banished opponents and freed his prisoners. The Pharisees avenged themselves on some of those who had supported Jannai's crucifixions. These measures induced resistance among the out-of-favor Sadducees, who then sought Aristobulus's support. To conciliate this faction and its growing numbers, Salome granted them control of several regional fortresses where they could settle. When she became terminally ill, it appeared that Aristobulus was preparing to take power. The alarmed Jewish elders, together with the high priest Hyrcanus, asked Salome's advice on dealing with the scheming rebels. The expiring queen merely advised them to do what they thought best, and died in 67 with no designated successor, after ruling nine years.[6]

On Salome's death Hyrcanus took the throne. Aristobulus marshaled his forces and defeated Hyrcanus's army near Jericho, when many of the latter's troops defected to him. He imprisoned Hyrcanus, and forced him to concede both the throne and the high priestly office. Hyrcanus's setback did not end the two brothers' rivalry, however, for a new figure, Antipater, an Idumean, came to his aid.

Antipater had been governor of Idumea under both Jannai and Salome. He rallied Hyrcanus's supporters, contacted the Nabataean king Aretas, and persuaded Hyrcanus to flee Jerusalem and place himself under Aretas's protection in Petra, the Nabataean capital. Aretas promised to reinstall Hyrcanus as Judean king, if he would surrender several cities east of the Jordan River which Jannai had taken from the Nabataeans. With Hyrcanus's agreement, Aretas marched into Judea and defeated Aristobulus when many of his troops fled to the Nabataeans. Aristobulus withdrew to the fortified temple precinct, where the priests supported him. Aretas besieged the temple with the populace's help, enhancing the likelihood that Hyrcanus would achieve the ascendancy Antipater sought for him. That this could be achieved only with the aid of the Nabataeans, Judea's traditional enemy, was an ominous development. It revealed the Hasmonean dynasty's vulnerable condition when Salome died leaving no strong successor; for, as her sons quarreled over the Judean throne, a new power was menacing the eastern Mediterranean.[7]

---

6. Josephus, *Ant.* 13.15.5; 13.16.1–6; Noth, *History of Israel*, 391.
7. Noth, *History of Israel*, 392–93.

VI

The Romans
Pompey, Julius Caesar, Mark Antony, and Octavian

DURING THE PREVIOUS TWO centuries the Roman Empire had expanded into the eastern Mediterranean. To deter the Seleucids from smothering the nascent Maccabean uprising, in 161, as we have seen, Judas Maccabaeus had wisely secured a mutual assistance pact with Rome, although it is doubtful that either signatory believed it would ever be activated. By the mid-first century BCE Roman power reached Palestine. After absorbing Mithridates's Pontic kingdom and Tigranes's Armenian domain, the Roman general Pompey moved to impose imperial authority on western Asia and liquidate the Seleucid Empire. In 65 he sent his legate Scaurus to Syria. On learning of the Aristobulus-Hyrcanus conflict, Scaurus went to Judea to investigate the matter. Both Judean aspirants offered him large bribes to secure his favor, but, believing that Aristobulus's prospects were more promising than Hyrcanus's, Scaurus confirmed Aristobulus in his offices and forced Aretas to lift his siege of Jerusalem and withdraw.[1]

When Pompey moved to Damascus in the spring of 63, regional delegations came seeking his favor. Aristobulus and Hyrcanus came in person, as did envoys from Judea, seemingly from Pharisaic circles, who wanted Hasmonean rule abolished and the high priestly office restored. Pompey promised to settle Judean affairs after completing a campaign against the Nabataeans. Impatient with Pompey's delay in resolving his conflict with

---

1. Noth, *History of Israel*, 402.

Hyrcanus, Aristobulus hastily returned to Judea and occupied the fortress at Alexandrium, presumably to strengthen his position. Vexed by Aristobulus's rash behavior, Pompey postponed the Nabataean campaign and ordered him to vacate the site. He complied and then moved on to Jerusalem to organize resistance there. Recognizing the futility of resisting Roman power, however, Aristobulus finally came to his senses, abandoned his reckless course of action, and went to Pompey's camp and agreed to hand over Jerusalem. Exercising caution, Pompey held Aristobulus and sent Gabinius to Jerusalem with troops to take possession of the city. When the inhabitants refused to admit Gabinius, the angered Pompey marched on the city with force. Jerusalem submitted, except for a minority of Aristobulus loyalists, who determined to defend the city from the fortified temple area. After a three-month siege Roman forces gained the temple and slaughtered its defenders. Pompey's presence in the temple, especially in the Holy of Holies, outraged the faithful, but he refrained from plundering it and soon permitted the resumption of sacrificial rituals. Hyrcanus was reappointed high priest, but Aristobulus and his two sons were sent to Rome as prisoners.[2]

Pompey's capture of the temple precinct in 63 was a turning point in ancient Israel's history, for it ended nearly eighty years of independence under the Maccabees. During the first century BCE the Maccabean state had grown to virtually equal Israel's dimensions during the glory days of David and Solomon. Ironically, however, the Hasmonean venture, undertaken to reestablish a theocratic state under the high priest's leadership in the second century, gradually succumbed in the first century to the very forces it was formed to guard against. By the degenerate Jannai's time, Judea was a corrupt hellenized kingdom virtually indistinguishable from neighboring states. Undoubtedly the Hyrcanus-Aristobulus struggle enfeebled the regime, but even had they not clashed over the throne following Salome's death, the Hasmoneans had little hope of maintaining their independence, for it rested on a weak foundation. Their rise to power had depended on a small group's support within a deeply divided society. By the first century the growing friction between the powerful land-rich aristocratic Sadducees and the less powerful Pharisees, not to mention the reclusive Essenes, had weakened the Judean social fabric. Lacking broad support, the Hasmoneans failed to establish a healthy, viable political structure, and increasingly relied on force to maintain their position. Nor did they develop a

2. Noth, *History of Israel*, 402–04.

peaceful method for transferring power to successive political leaders, as the Hyrcanus-Aristobulus struggle clearly showed. The overriding factor in the Hasmonean collapse, however, was the Roman Empire's dominance in the eastern Mediterranean by the mid-first century BCE. Nevertheless, the eighty-year Hasmonean interlude had a lasting impact on Jewish history. In the figure of Judas Maccabaeus future generations found a national hero to venerate, and the rededication of the temple in 164 following the withdrawal of Antiochus's Abomination of Desolation became an annual celebration—Hanukkah, the Festival of Lights—and remains a highlight in the Jewish cultural calendar.

Pompey extensively reorganized Syria-Palestine. The former Seleucid Empire's western region became the Roman province of Syria, and he separated the Hasmonean conquests in Palestine from Judea. He made the coastal cities independent urban Syrian communities, and the mainly Hellenistic cities the Hasmoneans had conquered in the central and northern area east of the Jordan became the Decapolis. The region of Samaria was assigned to Syria, while the city of Samaria, formerly a Macedonian military colony, became an independent Syrian city. The Jerusalem religious community's territory shrank to what had once been the old province of Judea, with the addition of Galilee, Idumea, and Perea (a strip of south-central land east of the Jordan) and was placed under the high priest, who answered to the Roman governor in Syria. Martin Noth, the twentieth-century Old Testament scholar, believed this was a fitting redistribution of territory, for it reflected the Jerusalem religious community's actual membership.[3]

In 57 Gabinius, the Syrian governor, hoping to stabilize Palestine, temporarily reorganized the Jerusalem community's affairs. He ended Hyrcanus's political authority, restricting his responsibilities to the high priest's religious duties. The community was divided into the five territories of Jerusalem, Gazara, Jericho, Perea (renamed the district of Amathus), and Galilee (renamed the district of Sepphoris) and was placed directly under the Syrian governor. This reconfiguration, however, fell short of its goal, for old antagonisms in Palestine along with instability in Rome precipitated a complicated interplay of intrigues as competing figures maneuvered for power. In Jerusalem a faction opposed Hyrcanus's retention of the high priestly office, while Aristobulus, still detained in Rome, schemed to regain the position Pompey had forced him to relinquish. He escaped and with his two sons assembled a force that moved against Hyrcanus, but Gabinius came to Hyrcanus's aid

---

3. Noth, *History of Israel*, 404–05.

and defeated Aristobulus, whom he returned to Rome as a prisoner. Following the failure of Aristobulus's venture, Gabinius cancelled his territorial redivision and returned the five districts to the high priest's control.[4]

Meanwhile, a struggle for power was brewing in Rome that affected Palestine. Julius Caesar, fresh from extending Rome's territory in western Europe, came into open conflict with Pompey, Rome's victorious general in the east, for the emperorship. When Caesar marched on Rome, Pompey fled east to gather forces, and Hyrcanus and Antipater backed him. Caesar planned to send Aristobulus, still imprisoned in Rome, east to participate in the coming battle, but Pompey's supporters poisoned him and soon murdered his son Alexander. In 48 Caesar defeated Pompey's forces at Pharsalus in Greece. He escaped to Egypt, where Caesar's agents soon assassinated him. With Caesar's victory Hyrcanus and Antipater, who had backed the defeated Pompey, urgently needed to be seen aligning themselves with the emperor. An opportunity soon came, when Caesar found himself militarily isolated in Egypt. Antipater dispatched troops to help him, while Hyrcanus persuaded the Jerusalem religious community to back Caesar.

Caesar lavishly rewarded Hyrcanus and Antipater when he visited Syria in 47. After confirming Hyrcanus as high priest, Caesar made him ethnarch (governor) of Judea, and named him a Roman "confederate." Jerusalem won full jurisdiction over its affairs, and Hyrcanus's territory gained exemption from making contributions to Rome and billeting soldiers in winter. For his part, Antipater received Roman citizenship, a coveted status, and was appointed procurator (chief administrative officer) of Judea. The strategic port of Joppa was restored to Judea, and Jews throughout the eastern Mediterranean were granted freedom and the right to worship freely.[5]

These remarkable concessions, more than merely generous rewards for the help Antipater's troops had given Caesar in Egypt, were significant. Deeply interested in the eastern portion of the Roman Empire, Caesar sought to conciliate its subject peoples to solidify his regional power base. Moreover, Antipater's new position enabled him to expand his interests, for, as procurator of Judea, he was in a position to advance the role of his two sons. He appointed Phasael to be *strategos* (administrator) of Judea and Perea, and made Herod *strategos* of Galilee.

Antipater's growing power aroused opposition in Jerusalem, especially within priestly and aristocratic circles, for they found his non-Jewish

---

4. Noth, *History of Israel*, 405–07.
5. Noth, *History of Israel*, 407–08.

Idumean roots objectionable. Events in Galilee soon offered them an opportunity to press Hyrcanus to restrain Antipater by moving against his son Herod. In his new capacity as administrator of Galilee, Herod had rounded up and summarily executed a band of Galilean thieves. The Jerusalem elite accused him of rashly overriding the Sanhedrin's authority, the assembly of priestly aristocracy and Pharisaic scribes that managed Jerusalem's internal affairs. Under duress, Hyrcanus summoned Herod to appear before the body. Strongly supported by the Syrian governor Sextus, who applauded his efforts to stamp out Galilean banditry, Herod defended himself so forcefully before the Sanhedrin that it avoided sentencing him. He secretly left Jerusalem only to reappear shortly outside the city with troops, seemingly intent on avenging his treatment. However, Antipater dissuaded him from retaliating against the Sanhedrin, and he returned to Galilee. The tension subsided without further trouble, but the incident was freighted with significance for the future. It was the Jerusalem leadership's first encounter with the shrewd and ambitious young Herod, who would eventually become Judea's formidable leader for three eventful decades.[6]

Meanwhile events in Rome were about to significantly affect Palestine; attention, therefore, must momentarily be focused on developments in the Roman Empire. When Julius Caesar defeated Pompey at Pharsalus in 48, it promised to calm Rome's previously troubled political atmosphere by resolving the pending question of the emperorship. Stability proved elusive, however, for in 44 a group of Caesar's aristocratic opponents assassinated him. Knowing how disruptive political succession could be to Roman political life, and seeking to avoid that contingency in the event of his own death, Caesar had named his great-nephew Octavian his heir. Following Caesar's death, the young Octavian, then serving in Illyrium, hastened to Rome to claim his inheritance, but this proved to be more difficult than he expected. It required forming an alliance against Caesar's assassins with two powerful figures, Mark Antony and Lepidus. This trio (the Triumvirate) succeeded in killing several of Caesar's murderers and seizing their property, but two, Brutus and Cassius, escaped to the east. Octavian and his cohorts eliminated them in 42 at the Battle of Phillippi (in Macedonia), and Roman power in the east devolved onto Mark Antony. (Eventually, one might almost say inevitably, Octavian and Mark Antony turned on each other in their respective pursuits of the emperorship. Octavian eventually succeeded in defeating the latter at Actium in 31 and gained the coveted

---

6. Noth, *History of Israel*, 409.

office. His long rule lasted until his death in 14 CE, but this is getting ahead of the story of events in Palestine.)

In 44, when Cassius fled east to escape the revenge-seeking Triumvirate, he became governor of Syria, exploited the province with high taxes, and was very unpopular. Antipater, Judea's procurator, who with High Priest Hyrcanus administered Judea, naturally sought to ingratiate himself with the Syrian governor, but his faithful service to Cassius further damaged his already tarnished reputation with the Jerusalem elite. Now Antipater was murdered in a conspiracy, implicating Hyrcanus. His death might have significantly weakened his sons' influence in Palestinian affairs, but Phasael and Herod, benefitting from Cassius's backing, were already securely entrenched in their positions. Herod shortly secured the execution of his father's murderer, and, if anything, Antipater's demise enhanced the brothers' positions.

At this juncture a new quest for Judean leadership—the matter, as we have seen, that had fueled the Hyrcanus/Aristobulus struggle—occurred. Antigonus, the murdered Aristobulus's remaining son, decided to claim the position he believed rightly belonged to him after his father's death. He invaded Galilee, but Herod defeated and expelled him; this gained Hyrcanus's goodwill, for he had never fully trusted Antipater and his ambitious sons. Grateful for Herod's protection, Hyrcanus persuaded him to become engaged to Mariamne, his Hasmonean grandniece and Aristobulus's granddaughter. Given his Idumean heritage, Herod undoubtedly hoped to enhance his connection with the Jerusalem community by marrying into Hasmonean royalty.

With Mark Antony now being governor of Syria, regional leaders naturally wanted his goodwill. Jerusalem delegations sought to prejudice him against Herod and Phasael, but when Herod went to Damascus and declared his loyalty, he won the powerful Roman's support. Herod and Phasael thus withstood the challenge to their growing influence inherent in Antipater's death by winning Mark Antony's backing, even though he was very unpopular because of the heavy tax burden he imposed.

Despite his defeat by Herod, Antigonus did not abandon hope of gaining power in Judea, and a second opportunity to reach his objective soon occurred. In 40 the Parthians, Syria's eastern neighbor, invaded the province, while Mark Antony was distracted by events in Rome, and by Queen Cleopatra, with whom he was spending time in Alexandria. In return for unspecified promises to the Parthians, Antigonus won their support in gaining his goal in Judea. With the Parthians occupied in northern Syria, Antigonus gathered supporters in Judea and forced his way into Jerusalem, where he encountered armed resistance from Herod and Phasael. Under pretext of settling the conflict between Herod/Phasael and Antigonus, the Parthians went to Jerusalem. They invited the brothers to their headquarters for talks, but Herod, suspecting a trap, declined. Phasael and Hyrcanus naively attended the meeting, and the duplicitous Parthians imprisoned them, and then installed Antigonus as king of Judea. When the Parthians released him to Antigonus, Phasael committed suicide. Hyrcanus's ears were cropped, disqualifying him for further service as high priest, and he was sent as a prisoner to Babylon. Antigonus continued as king of Judea for three years, but virtually nothing is known of his reign.[7]

---

7. Noth, *History of Israel*, 410–11.

VII

Herod

WITH HYRCANUS AND PHASAEL out of the way, Herod remained the only likely challenger to Antigonus's continued authority, for he was intent on gaining power in Judea. For their safety, Herod removed his family to Masada, the remote rocky pinnacle overlooking the Dead Sea's western shore, and left them there in his brother Joseph's care. Then, seeking help, he appealed to the Nabataeans, but they spurned his request. Undeterred by the Nabataeans' rebuff, and believing the Romans would welcome his support in removing Antigonus and their reconquest of Syria where the Parthians had installed him as king, he went to Rome. Relying on bribery and his negotiating skill, he won Mark Antony's support, who in turn gained Octavian's collaboration. With the approval of these two powerful figures, the senate obligingly appointed Herod king of Judea in 40 BCE.

Since Antigonus still held Judea, however, Herod had yet to gain actual possession of his kingdom. He went to Syria and found that Ventidius, the governor, had already ousted Antigonus and the Parthians, but left Antigonus in Judea. With Ventidius's help Herod occupied Joppa in 39, but when he laid siege to Jerusalem the effort failed, for Silo, Rome's second-in-command in Syria, withheld his assistance.[1] Herod then went to Galilee, presumably looking for help in his former bailiwick, but had no success, for the Parthians had reinvaded Syria. He finally appealed directly to Mark

1. Grant, *Herod*, 54.

Herod

Antony, then engaged in a siege on the upper Euphrates. His plea evidently succeeded, for on his return to Judea, Sosius, Syria's new governor, gave full support when he undertook Judea's conquest. Despite resistance from a faction of Jerusalem's elite, Herod and Sosius occupied the city in 37. The troops wreaked havoc in the city for a time, but when offered a bribe Sosius removed them, clearing the way for Herod to claim his royal office in Jerusalem. To ensure that Antigonus would not threaten Judea in the future, Herod had the Romans execute him in Antioch.[2]

With Antigonus gone and Jerusalem in his hands, the ambitious Herod gained control of Judea as a client king of the Romans. This was a demanding role, for it required sustaining a delicate balance between the interests of his Jewish kingdom and the demands of the Roman Empire. It proved to be a mutually advantageous arrangement. From the Roman perspective, it obviated the necessity of maintaining a costly Roman governor and his entourage, and by relying on Judeans to administer the kingdom, it undermined Jewish resistance to a foreign authority's presence. Moreover, holding Judea as a client kingdom rather than a Roman province was an efficient way to defend the empire's southeastern flank against the Nabataeans. In return for maintaining domestic order, raising the annual tribute, defending the border, and supplying Rome with troops and war materiel in times of crisis, Herod, as a client king, benefitted from the Roman Empire's protective umbrella. Otherwise, he was free to rule as he saw fit.

Implementing domestic order and advancing his kingdom's interests, however, was a daunting undertaking, for elements of Jerusalem's elite were hostile to him. Herod was a foreigner, of mixed Nabataean and Idumean heritage, and Judeans had long despised the Idumeans; for they were descendants of the Edomites, who in the distant past had refused Moses and the Israelites passage through their land during the Exodus from Egypt. Judeans also resented the Idumeans for welcoming their sixth-century Babylonian captivity, for it enabled the Idumeans to occupy territory in southern Judea.[3] Moreover, as we have seen, Hyrcanus (134–04) had annexed Idumea and forced Idumeans to accept circumcision and convert to Judaism, but in the eyes of Jewish nobility they scarcely merited even second-class citizenship. Jannai (103–76) had made Herod's grandfather (Antipater or Antipas, a hereditary Idumean chieftain) governor of Idumea. Much to the disapproval of the Jerusalem aristocrats, Herod's father (also named

---

2. Grant, *Herod*, 53–59.
3. Grant, *Herod*, 20.

Antipater), rose to be chief adviser to the high priest Hyrcanus. It was this group within the Jerusalem council that in 47 had summoned the young Herod, then *strategos* of Galilee, to answer for usurping council prerogatives by summarily executing the Galilean brigands he had captured. The same leaders had sided with Antigonus during Herod's siege of Jerusalem in 37. For them, it was unthinkable that Herod, Rome's Idumean appointee, should be king.

Herod moved quickly to check his upper-class opponents' influence by striking at the Jerusalem council. For resisting the opening of the city gates when he laid siege, he summarily executed forty-five council members, and seized their property. He ended the council's traditional judicial function, limiting its authority to settling doctrinal matters, and vested the council president's appointment—the high priest—in his own hands. There is no record of him consulting the council thereafter. These measures were a heavy blow to the Sadducees, the small select group who managed the temple's affairs, for many of them were council members. Apart from being large landowners, this group's entrenched position rested on their hereditary right to control the temple, for they were descendants of Zadok, the first high priest whom David had appointed. They claimed to be the written law's sole legitimate interpreters and regarded the temple's ceremonial rituals as more important than concern about personal morality or academic hairsplitting over the law's details and had no interest in the oral traditions. Herod's measures seriously damaged the interests of many wealthy and influential Judean magnates.[4]

Most of the councilors who escaped Herod's vengeance were Pharisees. They had emerged as a distinct group during the second century, and their religious outlook differed from that of the Sadducees. Pharisees believed that the law was Judaism's vital center. They held that at Sinai God had given Moses not only the written law, but, unlike the Sadducees, the unwritten law—the "Ancient Tradition," or the "Tradition of the Elders," as it was known in Herod's day. Pharisees saw it as their duty to preserve the law and hand it down to future generations. In contrast to the Sadducees, they stressed morality and personal religion, believed in resurrection of the body and an afterlife, and saw divine purpose in all history. Mainly members of the middle class, their strength lay in the synagogues of Judea's towns, where they studied and shaped Judean commoners' outlooks by teaching them the law in Aramaic, the language of ordinary Jews, for only

---

4. Grant, *Herod*, 61–62.

the educated understood Hebrew. To Sadducees, the Pharisees determined efforts to make the law relevant to national life and to Jews' daily activities, were vulgar appeals to the impressionable lower classes.

The Pharisees opposed the Hasmonean practice of merging the kingship and the high priestly office and the court's increasing hellenization. This had created friction with the Hasmoneans, but the tension dissipated markedly when Queen Salome (76–67) released the Pharisees her predecessor husband Jannai (103–76) had imprisoned. The Pharisees undoubtedly resented Rome's appointment of Herod, for it displaced the Hasmonean royal line. They recognized, however, that government was necessary to prevent humans from destroying each other, and, in their eyes, rule by Rome and Herod was God's judgment and must be endured. Hillel and Shammai, leaders in Jerusalem's Pharisaic academic circles, had favored opening the city gates during Herod's siege of the city, and when they advocated cooperating with the non-Hasmonean Herod, it would not have escaped his attention, and sheds light on his approbation of the Pharisees. They were prepared to tolerate Herod so long as he did not interfere with their religious practices.[5]

Jews disposed to according Herod a favorable, if limited, reception were also found within messianist circles. They anticipated a future golden age when Israel's former glory would be restored through divine intervention under the house of David's leadership. The belief was prevalent within Second Temple Judaism, and figures claiming to be the Messiah frequently appeared. Some wondered if the Hasmonean interlude might be the forerunner of this event. Old Testament scholars speculate that numerous monastic groups devoted to the belief—groups like the faction at Khirbet Qumran, for example—may have existed. This group had withdrawn into the Judean wilderness near the Dead Sea because of disagreement over how the Sadducee temple authorities were practicing the temple rituals. Scholars initially thought that these sectarians were Essenes, but recently Lawrence Schiffman has convincingly shown that the Qumran sectarians were not Essenes, but a breakaway sect of Sadducees.[6] The Essenes, possibly a second-century-BCE Pharisee offshoot, were devoted to meticulous conduct of ritual and interpretation of the Torah. Believing that all political leaders received their authority from God, they abjured resisting governing officialdom, although their opposition to the Hasmoneans is well known.

5. Grant, *Herod*, 62–66.
6. Schiffman, *Reclaiming the Dead Sea Scrolls*, 83–95.

These disparate groups were acceptable to Herod and they were inclined to side with those who welcomed him.[7]

Managing relations with these groups was an ongoing task Herod faced throughout his reign, but on assuming power his immediate problem was the thorny issue of filling the post of high priest. The office had been vacant since 40, when Antigonus had rendered Hyrcanus, the current high priest, unfit for further service by cropping his ears. Many expected Herod to name a Hasmonean royal family member to the office, and Aristobulus III, Hyrcanus's grandson and Herod's wife Mariamne's brother, was a possible choice, but as a teenager his youthfulness cast serious doubts on his suitability. Instead, Herod appointed the Babylonian Jew Ananel, a figure from an entirely different family. The choice reflected Herod's intention to keep control of the office in his own hands, for without local connections or loyalties Ananel would be inclined to accommodate Herod's wishes. Herod also ended the office's heritability and lifetime tenure, and lodged its robes in his palace, allowing their removal only for the three yearly festivals of Passover, Pentecost, and Tabernacles and the Day of Atonement. Ananel's appointment was also a calculated move to check Hasmonean influence, for Ananel belonged to Zadok's priestly line, which meant he clearly outranked the Hasmoneans, who traced their lineage to an obscure priestly clan.

Herod's shrewd maneuver, however, was counterproductive, for it aroused opposition from a formidable member of the Hasmonean family. Alexandra II—the former high priest Hyrcanus's daughter and Herod's mother-in-law—wanted the high priesthood for her son Aristobulus III and was angered by Herod's appointment of Ananel. She urged her friend Cleopatra, the Egyptian queen, to convince Mark Antony, her lover, to direct Herod to replace Ananel with Aristobulus. A descendant of Egypt's Ptolemaic rulers, Cleopatra hoped to restore Palestine to Egyptian control as in the distant past, and she pressed Mark Antony to accommodate her wish. Antony, however, saw Palestine, in Herod's capable hands, as the key to defending the Roman Empire's southeastern flank, and eschewed sacrificing him to Cleopatra's request. Instead, he convinced Herod to assuage the Egyptian queen by ceding territory to her that included a strip of the Phoenician coast and much of Palestine's Mediterranean coastline. Herod was also forced to grant Cleopatra the valuable date palms and balsam-producing trees near Jericho, which he then leased back from her at considerable expense. The Alexandra-Cleopatra nexus was clearly a threat to

---

7. Grant, *Herod*, 66–72.

Herod, for Antony's desire to please Cleopatra might lead him to require additional Judean concessions to her. Wanting to avoid endangering his all-important relationship with Antony, Herod, much to his displeasure, acceded to Alexandra's wish; he deposed Ananel and appointed seventeen-year-old Aristobulus high priest in 36.

Having been forced to accommodate Alexandra, Herod kept close watch on her. Suspecting that she might scheme to overthrow him, she was confined to her palace. Undeterred, Alexandra again appealed to Cleopatra, who advised fleeing to Egypt with Aristobulus. When their flight was intercepted midway, Herod feigned graciously forgiving the misadventure. However, when shortly thereafter a crowd warmly applauded Aristobulus while participating in the Feast of Tabernacles, Herod determined to rid himself of the young Hasmonean high priest and arranged his drowning in an apparent pool accident in Jericho, where the young man was being entertained in 36.[8]

Although Aristobulus was given an elaborate funeral, Alexandra did not believe his death was accidental. Angry and sorrowful, she again appealed to Cleopatra, who managed to convince Antony to summon Herod, presumably to answer for what had happened to Aristobulus. Having just returned to Syria from an inconclusive campaign against the Parthians, Antony's focus was on securing Syria's eastern border rather than settling the petty scandals of Herod's court. Antony summoned Herod to Laodicea, but much to Alexandra and Cleopatra's displeasure, rather than requiring him to explain Aristobulus's death as they expected, Herod was invited to join Antony on a tribunal to adjudicate several cases then coming before him. To placate Cleopatra, Antony advised Herod to cede her the Gaza Strip. Herod complied, thereby completing Cleopatra's control of the entire Palestinian coastline and leaving the Judean kingdom landlocked.[9]

While these domestic concerns dominated his early years, Herod had to be alert to developments in Rome, for events there could profoundly affect the empire's remote corners, requiring a client king like Herod to trim his sails carefully in order to maintain good relations with the empire's center. Herod had aligned himself with Mark Antony, the powerful general who controlled the empire's eastern half, while Octavian dominated the west. Both men were intent on gaining the emperorship. Their competition for the grand prize came to a head in 31 with the naval Battle of Actium off

8. Grant, *Herod*, 75–82.
9. Grant, *Herod*, 82.

Greece's east coast, where Octavian defeated Antony and Cleopatra's combined forces. The victory opened the door for Octavian to become emperor.

Herod had loyally supported Antony during the long struggle, and he faced the necessity of reconciling with the new emperor. An opportunity to induce reconciliation conveniently occurred when, following their defeat at Actium, Antony and Cleopatra fled to Egypt. Needing to strengthen their garrison, they ordered a small group of gladiators in Asia Minor to come to Egypt. Syria's Roman governor had already switched sides to Octavian, and Herod seized the chance to promote his own rapprochement with Octavian by helping the Syrian governor intercept the gladiator detachment on its way to Egypt.

In view of his past allegiance to Antony, Herod feared that Octavian might appoint a representative of the Hasmonean dynasty to replace him as Judean king. Hyrcanus II, the former ethnarch, high priest, and king, was a likely choice, for Herod had allowed him to return to Jerusalem from captivity in Babylon. To remove him as a threat, Herod shrewdly concocted the story that Hyrcanus was plotting with a neighboring Arab monarch to seize Judea and become king again; then Herod had him strangled.

To placate Octavian and appeal for reconciliation, Herod planned to meet him in Rhodes. He was concerned, however, that in his absence Alexandra and her daughter Mariamne, his second wife, might lead a Hasmonean revolt. To prevent this, before leaving, he confined them in Fortress Alexandriun, and to doubly ensure against their scheming, he sent his children by Mariamne to Masada as hostages of his brother Pheroras. He further ordered that if he did not return, to prevent them from seizing power and save the kingship for his children, Alexandra and Mariamne were to be executed.[10]

With these arrangements in place, Herod went to Rhodes and met Octavian in the spring of 30. Tactfully removing his crown before the emperor, Herod acknowledged having supported Antony, but vowed his loyalty to Octavian. Convinced he would be a reliable ally, Octavian confirmed Herod's kingship. A timely opportunity to demonstrate his support was conveniently at hand, for Octavian was preparing a campaign to eliminate Antony and Cleopatra and annex Egypt, where, as we have seen, they had fled following their defeat at Actium. Herod offered accommodation and war supplies as Octavian advanced toward Egypt and joined the expedition. When Antony and Cleopatra committed suicide, Octavian returned

---

10. Grant, *Herod*, 90–94.

to Herod the territories Antony had forced him to give the Egyptian queen. The emperor further rewarded Herod by granting him two towns in the Decapolis, the area southeast of the Sea of Galilee. Changing allegiance from Antony to Octavian was a challenging task fraught with danger, for as a client king Herod served at Octavian's pleasure and could be removed at any time. He handled this delicate transition with consummate skill, however, gained Octavian's confidence, and won an expansion of his kingdom. Like all client monarchs Herod would be required to help Rome when aid was requested, and provide the annual tributes, but otherwise he was free to manage his internal affairs.[11]

Developments on the northern border later in the decade further enlarged Herod's kingdom. Iturea, a principality northeast of the Sea of Galilee, was ruled by the undisciplined monarch Zenodorus, whose Arab subjects had a reputation for brigandage. Zenodorus aroused Syrian anger for allowing Itureans to plunder the commerce of Damascus traders. After the merchants' repeated appeals to Syrian governors, in 23 BCE Augustus, the title Octavian had received from the senate, ordered Zenódorus to cede Trachonitis, Batanaea, and Aurantis, areas northeast of the Sea of Galilee, to Herod,[12] believing presumably that Herod would eradicate the Itureans' pillaging. Following Zenodorus's death three years later, Augustus granted Herod two additional territories—Ulatha and Panias—on the Syrian border.[13] Undoubtedly Augustus wanted these border regions under Herod's reliable control rather than in the hands of an untrustworthy Iturean prince. With these five additional territories, all of "traditional, historic Israel" was in Herod's hands, something no Jew had achieved since the time of Solomon.[14]

Herod's reconciliation with Augustus aroused consternation among Jews who opposed Rome, while serious domestic conflict soon beset his family. Alexandra and Mariamne harbored grudges for the murders of Hyrcanus and Aristobulus, and family tension must have intensified when they learned that Herod had ordered their killing if he did not return from Rhodes. Alexandra had additional grounds for resentment in the loss of Cleopatra, her friend and confidante, as a result of Augustus's Egyptian campaign in which Herod had participated. Herod's sister Salome, whom Mariamne and Alexandra despised because she was Idumean, exacerbated

11. Grant, *Herod*, 96–98.
12. Grant, *Herod*, 137–38.
13. Grant, *Herod*, 146–47.
14. Grant, *Herod*, 147.

matters further by insinuating that they were leading an anti-Herod Hasmonean plot. Fearing a coup, Herod imprisoned Mariamne, and when tortured witnesses convinced him she was culpable, he executed her in 29.

Mariamne's death engulfed Herod in a wave of remorse and guilt, heightened by a severe outbreak of boils, and he suffered a nervous collapse. Meanwhile Alexandra, in a vulnerable position with little to lose, asserted her claim to the throne as a member of the Hasmonean royal family. With Herod incapacitated in Samaria by his depressed condition, she invited two Jerusalem fortress commanders to seize the opportunity to revolt. Instead, they loyally informed Herod of his mother-in-law's treachery. He ordered her execution for treason, after which he quickly recovered.

Alexandra's death did not end Herod's anxiety over the Hasmonean menace, however, for the behavior of one of his own Idumean countrymen soon reawakened his smoldering suspicion. Castobarus, governor of Idumea, had narrowly escaped implication in a plot to restore Idumean independence when Herod's sister Salome intervened on his behalf. After Salome's husband was executed for malpractices during Herod's absence in Rhodes, she married Castobarus. Following Alexandra's execution in 28 or 27, there was new information casting fresh doubt on Castobarus's loyalty. Herod had assigned him the task of hunting down his opponents among the noble Jews who, as we have seen, were executed for opposing his entry into Jerusalem, but rather than dutifully fulfilling this task Castobarus had secretly hidden two Hasmonean youths. Following a domestic quarrel, Salome divorced Castobarus and revealed the two Hasmonean youths' existence to Herod. This made Castobarus a traitor in Herod's eyes, and he executed him and his associates before hunting down and killing the two Hasmonean youths.[15]

Having disposed of the supposedly disloyal Castobarus, and there being no males remaining in the royal family, the Hasmonean threat finally ceased. With these domestic concerns resolved, Herod could return to managing relations with Rome, a matter requiring great vigilance throughout his entire reign. Octavian's victory over Mark Antony at Actium was the occasion of great celebration in Rome. Herod, the erstwhile Antony supporter, having reconciled with Octavian, was anxious to show his loyalty to the Roman Empire by joining the celebration. This undoubtedly accounts for his large contribution to Nicopolis, the new town Rome was building near Actium to commemorate the battle. Wanting Jerusalem also to be seen

---

15. Grant, *Herod*, 98–101.

honoring Octavian's triumph, he instituted the Actian Games in 28 or 27. Modeled after the Greek Olympiad, the celebrations—racing, theatrical, musical, and athletic competitions and deadly wild animal fights—were to occur every four years at Jerusalem.

Although Rome undoubtedly welcomed the Actian Games, they aroused resistance in Jerusalem. Unlike Greeks and Romans, the Judeans had little taste for athletics, and conservative Jews viewed the games as an unwelcome drift toward Hellenism. To house the games, three separate sites were constructed. A hippodrome for chariot racing was built within the city adjacent to the temple, but to accommodate Hasidim sensitivities the theater and amphitheater were located outside Jerusalem's walls. Theater attendance was not specifically forbidden by the Torah, but the bloody gladiatorial displays, so popular in Rome, must have distressed Jews. It was wrestling and gymnastics, however, that were most offensive to them, for they deplored the competitors' nudity. Circumcised visitors to gymnasiums were jeered and often embarrassed, leading some to undergo surgery to reverse circumcision. This scandalized conservative Jews, for in their eyes the rite symbolized membership in the religious community, and its reversal constituted repudiation of the covenant, the divine promise that anchored Jewish religious belief.

There was a further problem with the Actian Games. Herod wished the structures housing the events to be as fine as possible. However, they could not be fitted with the statuary that was characteristic of public buildings elsewhere throughout the Mediterranean world, for the law forbade graven images. To avoid violating this stricture, the sites were adorned with trophies and weapons, but religious Jews were still offended, for they believed Romans worshipped these symbols. The Actian Games and their accoutrements awakened such intense feelings that an attempt was made to assassinate Herod, but his intelligence network discovered the plot and the conspirators were caught and executed. Thereafter resistance to Herod went underground, where it remained until late in his reign.[16]

The assassination plot raised doubts about Jerusalem's loyalty to him, however, and to relieve this concern and shore up his domestic security Herod strengthened the ancient city of Samaria that lay to the north of Jerusalem. Samaria had been the northern kingdom's capital prior to its capture by Assyria, and following Alexander's late-fourth-century campaign, it became a military colony for soldiers retiring from his army and settlers from Greece

---

16. Grant, *Herod*, 103–05.

and Macedonia. Hyrcanus I (134–04) virtually destroyed it in 107 during his expansionist military campaigns, and a half-century later Samaria became an independent urban enclave during Pompey's time. Augustus included it in his territorial grant to Herod at their post-Actium reconciliation.[17] Beginning in 27, Herod rebuilt it on a massive scale, renaming it "Sebaste," Greek for "Augustus." Protected by gated walls, the site with its intersecting streets covered one hundred and sixty acres. An agora facilitated trade, and aqueducts supplied water, while a theater and hippodrome provided entertainment, and the Temple of Roma and Augustus accommodated the imperial cult. To promote the surrounding area's growth, Herod distributed choice lots of land to attract settlers who in return were subject to military service in a special corps, half of whose members came from the settlement. By this means Herod cleverly created a reliable military force near Jerusalem he could call on should the need arise. Jerusalem's residents, however, saw Sebaste as a fortress to dominate Judea.[18]

The refurbishing of Sebaste—a seventeen-year undertaking—is only one example of the vast building program that was a hallmark of Herod's monarchy. The projects ranged from founding new cities to constructing fortresses and palaces, religious and cultural buildings, commercial sites and infrastructure. They were spread throughout the eastern portion of the Roman Empire from Epirus in western Greece to Idumea in the southeast, but were concentrated in Jerusalem and Judea. They are known today through the archaeological work done on their remains, their significance as examples of Second Temple Jewish structures, and from references in ancient literary sources. In the judgment of Herod scholar and architectural critic Peter Richardson, the structures are "stunning in their size, boldness, and complexity."[19]

Among Herod's dramatic projects were the new cities he founded. Rebuilding Sebaste was a remarkable achievement, but his showpiece, Caesarea Maritima on the Mediterranean coast near the Syrian border, surpassed it in complexity and importance. He began its construction at the ancient site called Strato's Tower in 22 BCE. Protected by a lengthy seawall, the capacity of its twenty-fathom-deep harbor rivaled any other in the entire Mediterranean basin, even the Piraeus that served Athens. The city covered one hundred and sixty-four acres and housed a cosmopolitan

17. Noth, *History of Israel*, 231, 346, 387, 404, 414.
18. Grant, *Herod*, 106–10; Richardson, *Herod*, 179.
19. Richardson, *Herod*, 174–77.

population of approximately fifty thousand Jews, Greeks, Romans, Egyptians, and Nabataeans. It contained an agora, hippodrome, theater, amphitheater, palace, and a Temple of Roma and Augustus to accommodate the imperial cult. The city opened officially in 10 BCE with magnificent games funded by the emperor.[20]

Caesarea Maritima and Sebaste were only the most prominent examples of Herod's new cities, for he also founded or rebuilt other less-grand yet significant towns. In the southwest near Gaza, for example, he restored Agrippias, while Antipatris, a new town named after his father, sat astride the main trade route linking Jerusalem and Caesarea Maritima, and Phasaelis, north of Jericho, honored his brother Phasael. Close to extensive royal estates, these sites were likely intended to stimulate agriculture and trade and enrich the royal coffers.

Herod also established military settlements where demobilized veterans received land. Gaba was located northeast of Caesarea Maritima near the Syrian border, and Pente Komai ("Five Villages") was a military site with six thousand settlers north of Sebaste. Across the Jordan there were similar installations at Heshbon in Perea and Bathyra in Batanea. A combination of need, availability of land, and strategic considerations determined these military settlements' locations.[21]

Herod provided these sites with numerous cultural structures. Theaters, amphitheaters, hippodromes, stadiums, public baths, and gymnasiums were foreign to Jews, but they accommodated the customs of hellenized populations and usually were built where they were the majority. At these sites dramatic performances, games, and athletic competitions occurred and philosophy was studied. Jerusalem's conservative Jews were especially sensitive about such activities, although it had a gymnasium even before the Hasmonean rebellion. Herod added a theater and an amphitheater or hippodrome—possibly both—but out of respect for local sensibilities located them outside the city. He built similar facilities in Jericho, Caesarea Maritima, Sebaste, and Herodium. Askelon received a public bath, while in Syria Ptolemais, Tripolis, and Damascus gained gymnasiums, and theaters were built at Sidon and the capital.[22]

Herod also expanded Palestine's commercial life with his building program. The clearest evidence of this is the great port he built at Caesarea

---

20. Grant, *Herod*, 167–70; Richardson, *Herod*, 177–79; Noth, *History of Israel*, 415.
21. Grant, *Herod*, 114; Richardson, *Herod*, 177–78.
22. Richardson, *Herod*, 186–88.

Maritima. With its deep-water harbor, extensive wharfage and warehousing capacity connected by underground passages, it was the natural maritime outlet for Samaria and Sebaste; it became the home base of the Judean navy and was a commercial center comparable to Alexandria that reconfigured regional trading patterns. He constructed agoras (marketplaces) at smaller sites like Agrippias, Antipatris, and Phasaelis. Beyond Judea he provided similar facilities for Tyre and Berytus (Beirut). In Antioch he paved the main street and fitted it with colonnades, and at Chios, on an Aegean island southwest of Turkey, rebuilt a stoa—a covered market open on one side—along the city wall. He also assisted Rhodes's shipbuilding industry, a supplier of vessels for the Judean navy.[23]

To guard against rebellion and increase border security, Herod built new fortresses and refurbished his predecessors' existing strongholds. Wishing to avoid lodging the royal household in the Acra, his Hasmonean opponents' traditional Jerusalem residence, Herod built a new fortress palace in the city early in his reign (37–35); named the Antonia after Mark Antony, then his Roman patron, it was strategically located next to the temple to facilitate riot control in the adjacent precinct should outbreaks occur. Hyrcania, a military site Hyrcanus constructed southeast of Jerusalem near the Dead Sea, was rebuilt; it became known as a place from which captives never returned. On the western shore of the Dead Sea, Masada was fortified, and the Alexandrium, which Jannai had founded on a mountain top overlooking the Jordan Valley near the river's confluence with the Jabbok River, was rebuilt to protect trade between Samaria and Jericho. Cypros, named in honor of his mother, shielded Jericho, while the new fortress at Machaerus and the Eastern Herodium guarded the eastern border. Herod intended the great Western Herodium ultimately to be his mausoleum site, but its immediate purpose was to keep Jerusalem quiet. These military installations quartered Judean conscripts, Idumean mercenaries, and Greeks, Thracians, Germans, and Galatians from Cleopatra's troops who were transferred to Herod after her death.[24]

Herod also spent lavishly on palaces for himself. As we have seen, early in his reign he moved the royal family into the Antonia, but it was primarily a fortress for securing the city and lacked the grandeur befitting a royal palace. Accordingly in 23 Herod began building a third palace in Jerusalem; situated on the western ridge overlooking the city, and twice the

---

23. Grant, *Herod*, 167–70; Richardson, *Herod*, 188–89.
24. Grant, *Herod*, 73–75, 85, 110–15; Richardson, *Herod*, 97.

size of the Antonia, it was strategically located to impress the population. Should the need arise, it could signal other area fortresses, a capability lacking at the Antonia because of the surrounding hills. Ever conscious of the need to ensure Rome's favor, Herod outfitted the palace with apartments for Augustus and Marcus Agrippa, his deputy. The winter palace at Jericho was near the Cypros fortress and a lush oasis renowned for its date palms, balsam groves, and bountiful supply of fruits and vegetables. Built astride a wadi, with a fine villa on one side connected by a bridge to a tiered water-garden on the other, like its Jerusalem counterpart it contained apartments for Augustus and Marcus Agrippa.[25]

Not content with palaces in Jerusalem and Jericho, Herod built royal residences elsewhere, possibly to impress outlying Judeans with his government's authority. In Galilee there was a palace at Sepphoris, and another lay across the Jordan in Perea, six miles north of the Dead Sea at Betharamphtha. Near the sea's south end in Idumea, there were royal residences at opposite ends of Masada's bleak hilltop fortress. Herod also had palaces beyond the kingdom, at Ascalon, Idumea's natural port, and Antioch, the gift of a Syrian governor.[26]

Numerous and serving a variety of purposes, Herod's construction projects were progressive in character and employed advanced techniques as in the water and sewerage systems of cities like Caesarea Maritima and Jerusalem. The former's water came from a source at the base of Mount Carmel twenty-two kilometers to the north along a newly-built aqueduct. Its sewerage, an engineering marvel, relied on the Mediterranean's rising and falling tides to flush the city's waste. In Jerusalem he built several large reservoirs to supply water: the Pool of Israel (north of the temple), the Struthion Pool for the Antonia, the Mamillah Pool (northwest of the Jaffa Gate), Hezekiah's Pool (northeast of the Jaffa Gate), and the Sheep Pool. Most were above the temple platform's level and could supply water for cultic needs as well as the general population. Herod's most elaborate water project was supplying Solomon's Pool: collected in a bowl-shaped basin south of Bethlehem, it flowed to Jerusalem along a twenty-four-kilometer aqueduct. To handle the great volume of blood and waste the sacrifices produced, his engineers constructed an elaborate drainage system under the temple.

---

25. Grant, *Herod*, 125–30.
26. Grant, *Herod*, 132–36.

Similar arrangements of aqueducts, collection basins, pools and reservoirs, and drainage facilities, were characteristic of many Herodian cities.[27]

In addition to stately residences, powerful fortresses, commercial infrastructure, and cultural facilities for popular entertainment, Herod built numerous religious structures throughout Judea and beyond. We have noted the temples of Roma and Augustus at Sebasta and Caesarea Maritima. There was a third temple for the imperial cult at Panias north of the Sea of Galilee near the Syrian border. These buildings expressed Herod's loyalty to Rome. The hellenized sites where they were located undoubtedly were chosen carefully to avoid offending Jews, but while Jews lived at these locations, surprisingly, they offered no opposition. In all likelihood they regarded the temples as extensions of Jerusalem's customary practice of offering daily prayers and sacrifices on the emperor's behalf. Herod, it seems, also helped finance a temple of Ba'al Shamim near Canatha in Aurantis to accommodate Nabataean religious interests.[28]

Herod also lavished attention on religious sites in Idumea. The province, as we have noted, was a late addition to the Judean kingdom, but Hebron, its capital, held special meaning for Jews because of its association with iconic figures from Israel's distant past. Abraham, Sarah, Jacob, Rachel, and Leah were buried there at the Machpelah Caves, and Hebron was David's capital before he captured Jerusalem. With Idumea safe from rebellion following Castobarus's death, Herod raised a grand memorial for these revered progenitors by surrounding their tombs with a great wall. Close by at Mamre, where Abraham had pitched his tent and raised an altar on returning from Egypt, Herod rebuilt and enclosed an earlier monument. Undoubtedly, he intended these sites, so grandly celebrating Israel's historic figures, to strengthen his connection with Israel's tradition, ingratiate him with his subjects, and promote the kingdom's unity and strength.[29]

Josephus, the first-century-CE historian, claims that Herod's religious buildings are also found at sites beyond his kingdom. These included temples at Tyre and Berytus and the Temple of Pythian Apollo on the island of Rhodes. Herod may also have contributed to restoring the religious structures at Olympia in Greece, damaged by an earthquake in 36 BCE.[30]

---

27. Richardson, *Herod*, 189–91.
28. Richardson, *Herod*, 184.
29. Gen 13:18; 23:1–20; 25:7–10; 49:29–33; 2 Sam 5:1–5; Grant, *Herod*, 101–03.
30. Richardson, *Herod*, 185; Josephus, *War* 1.21.11; *Ant.* 16.5.3.

Toward the end of his reign's second decade, Herod launched what he regarded as the culminating project of his life's work—the reconstruction of the Second Temple. As we have seen, Nebuchadnezzar destroyed Solomon's temple in 586. Zerubbabel's temple, the Second Temple, a more modest structure built following the Judeans' return Babylon, was desecrated by Antiochus IV Epiphanes preceding the Hasmonean rebellion, but Judas Maccabaeus cleansed and rededicated it in 164. To Herod, however, the Second Temple seemed inadequate for Israel's restored greatness in his day, and he decided to replace it with a more appropriate edifice. It would be the "most glorious of all his actions . . . sufficient for an everlasting memorial of him"[31] and end "misunderstandings about him among his Jewish subjects,"[32] while leaving "Judaism richer for him having been king."[33]

To allay possible suspicion about what might be his ulterior motive, Herod announced his intention to rebuild the temple at a public meeting in 22, and he published the building plans before demolition of the existing temple began. It would be virtually twice the First Temple's size, and the chief building material would be the same white stone used in the original temple from Solomon's nearby quarries. The workforce would consist of ten thousand men, a thousand of whom would be priests trained in carpentry and masonry, for the law restricted laymen's movement within the temple.

Five wards made up the temple: the Courts of Gentiles, Women, Israel, Priests, and the Sanctuary. The Court of Gentiles, a thirty-five-acre paved rectangle, enclosed the other four within a wall. The Antonia Fortress occupied the northwest corner, while there was a single gate on the north wall, two on each of the east and south walls, and three on the west. A double row of Greco-Roman Corinthian columns surrounded the court's interior on three sides. The most famous of these colonnades located on the east side was called Solomon's Porch, for it was an enlarged version of a portico from the First Temple's time. (Solomon's Porch is mentioned three times in the New Testament—John 10:23; Acts 3:11; and Acts 5:12.) A triple-rowed colonnade on the south side was known as the Royal Porch; tradition claimed it marked the site of Solomon's coronation. The court's colonnade enclosed spaces for dealers of many kinds, money changers, storerooms, a bakehouse for the loaves of showbread, money chests for offerings, administrative offices, and a chamber where the council met. On

---

31. Josephus, *Ant.* 15.11.1
32. Richardson, *Herod*, 185.
33. Grant, *Herod*, 150–52.

pain of death, non-Jews could not enter the temple complex beyond the Court of Gentiles.[34]

Beyond the Court of Gentiles was the Court of Women, surrounded by a fence or grating. One entered through three gates, the largest of which—the Corinthian Gate—was located on the east side. It was in this court that Mary and Joseph presented the infant Jesus in keeping with the law's requirements (Luke 2:22). This precinct was as far as women were permitted in the temple.[35]

The Court of Women led to the Court of Israel (or the Court of Men) through a magnificent gate approached by fifteen semi-circular steps on its west side. Every male Jew had access to this enclosure.[36]

On its west side this court joined the Court of Priests. In this cincture immediately before the Sanctuary stood the Altar of Burnt Offering, a large cubical structure of unhewn stone, approached by a ramp. Tradition held that this was where Abraham intended to sacrifice Isaac and where David was commanded to build an altar to the Lord on the site of the threshing floor of Ornan of the Jebusites, Jerusalem's occupants before the Israelites arrived (2 Chr 21:18).[37]

Just beyond the altar were twelve steps leading up to the Sanctuary, a tall three-stage structure with massive white walls. From the first stage, the Porch, one entered the second, the Holy Place, through tall doors at the back faced with precious metals. The Holy Place housed the Table of Shewbread, the lampstand holding the Menorah—the seven-branched candlestick—and the Altar of Incense. Separating the Holy Place from the Sanctuary's third compartment, the Holy of Holies, were two curtains, called the Veil of the Temple, hung between the building's walls. The Holy of Holies held the Ark of the Covenant, the chest containing the Ten Commandments. Only the high priest entered this compartment. This he did once a year on Yom Kipur, the Day of Atonement ("God's Great Pardon").

The Sanctuary was completed in 18 BCE amidst great celebration, but construction of the other courtyards continued for another ten years, while the temple complex's outer wall was not completed until 63 CE.[38]

---

34. Grant, *Herod*, 153–58.
35. Grant, *Herod*, 158.
36. Grant, *Herod*, 158–59.
37. Grant, *Herod*, 159–61.
38. Grant, *Herod*, 161–64.

Perhaps the most remarkable aspect of Herod's building program is its "almost overpowering" extent. One list of its projects covers five pages. It might be assumed that Herod launched this herculean undertaking as a megalomaniac, driven by visions of personal grandeur. Herod scholar Peter Richardson dismisses this explanation, however, for its simplicity. He insists that the forces behind the program were complex and changed as Herod's needs and circumstances changed.[39]

In the thirties BCE, when Herod initially claimed power, his roots in Israel's cultural soil were still shallow because of his Idumean-Nabataean heritage. He needed to consolidate his position. The general population, as we have seen, was ill-disposed toward him, and Antigonus remained a threat to regain the crown Herod had wrenched from him with Roman help in 37. The Nabataeans were a hostile presence on the eastern border, and to check them Herod refurbished fortresses built during the Hasmonean era along that frontier. These were not only strategic defensive installations but sites where he could find personal safety should the need arise.[40] Defense and self-preservation were both at play in his building projects during his reign's early years, but the self-preservation motive should not be stressed unduly, for Herod was not a king who controlled his subjects by force of arms and well-manned forts.

Herod lived in a patronage-dominated Roman world that placed high value on winning honor and showing gratitude. One was expected to show his patrons gratefulness, and accrue honor, by spending large sums memorializing individuals or communities that had been helpful. These considerations were clearly evident as Herod's building program developed. While going to Rome for help in dislodging Antigonus from the Judean throne in 40, interests on the Mediterranean island of Rhodes off the southwest cost of Asia Minor had assisted Herod. After becoming king, he rewarded the island (part of the Roman Province of Asia in Asia Minor) with funds for its ship-building industry and contracts from the Judean navy. The Jerusalem fortress he built in the mid-thirties, as we have seen, was named the Antonia for Mark Antony, the powerful benefactor who had sponsored his case in Rome. As we have seen, after refurbishing Samaria in the following decade he named it Sebaste, the Greek term for "Augustus," Rome's new emperor. In both instances Herod used his building projects to show gratitude and win honor.

---

39. This analysis of the reasons behind Herod's building program draws extensively on Richardson, *Herod*, 192-96.

40. Noth, *History of Israel*, 416-17.

By the late thirties Herod had reached a promising accommodation with Octavian and improved his position in Judea. Advancing his kingdom's economic wellbeing now seemingly became a key factor behind his building projects. In the early twenties, with work on Masada, the theater and amphitheater in Jerusalem, and several other sites already underway, he launched a massive expansion of his building program. The construction began at Sebaste in 27, and work at Caesarea Maritima, Herodium, the temple, and several other palaces and fortresses soon followed. The building accelerated through the late twenties until a "staggering" number of projects were underway simultaneously.[41]

The work lasted well into Herod's later years. Whether Herod consciously launched this vast undertaking to enhance trade and promote Judean economic expansion is questionable. Such a claim has a suspiciously modern ring, for it would require him to have had a surprising level of theoretical economic sophistication for the time. This enormous volume of construction undoubtedly boosted employment, enhanced trade, and accelerated Judean economic growth.

While Herod's building program benefited the Judean economy, he never lost sight of the kingdom's client status. Wisdom dictated the necessity of giving careful attention to accommodating the Roman Empire if Judea was to thrive and he was to remain king. Following his defeat of Antony in 31, the young Octavian quickly rose to undisputed leadership of the empire. In 27 he proposed reforms for the empire's better governance, and the grateful senate acclaimed him emperor with the title "Augustus," a cognomen carrying implications of majesty and holiness. It elevated him to become the object of worship within the imperial cult, a public rite involving veneration of the emperor and the goddess Roma. This spurred the cult's growth, especially in the east. Herod might have avoided this movement, for the Jews were well-known monotheists, and probably few would have expected Judea to violate its strongly-held religious traditions by practicing the imperial cult. Nevertheless, Herod accommodated it. He built temples of Augustus and Roma at Sebaste, Caesarea Maritima, and Panias, locations where there was likely to be minimal resistance. These sites for practicing the imperial cult symbolized reverence for the emperor and Roman traditions; given Judea's client-kingdom status, this was a pragmatic demonstration of respect for imperial piety.

---

41. For a comprehensive list of Herod's building projects, see Richardson, *Herod*, 197–203.

The building program also reveals Herod's wish to evince Jewish piety, which would benefit him personally, for as a latecomer to the Judean community he needed to burnish his Jewish credentials. Suspicions about him lingered in the public mind, extending even to his legitimacy as king. Constructing the elaborate memorial at the ancestral Israelite burial site in Hebron at the Malpech Caves and Mamre was an early effort to identify with Jewish tradition. It was the temple's reconstruction, however—the crowning glory of his life's work—that was his ultimate expression of Jewish piety, and he managed the project with great care. To allay fears of his possibly nefarious intentions, he announced his plans, as we have seen, well in advance, taking care to explain that temple ritual would continue undisturbed and that specially trained priests would carry out strategic portions of the work to avoid defiling the edifice. The undertaking was a magnificent success in its own right, ensuring Herod's lasting place in Jewish history. Influential Jews lavished their praise, declaring, "He who has not seen Herod's temple has not seen beauty."[42]

Herod adapted his building program to accommodate the social customs of the hellenized segment of Judean society, and buildings in Jerusalem, Sebaste, and Caesarea Maritima reflected this. Gymnasiums and hippodromes were places to watch and participate in athletic events, while theaters and amphitheaters facilitated dramatic performances and musical and oratorical competitions; all were valued activities in Greek life. Doric and Corinthian pillars, architectural features of Greek provenance, frequently graced Herod's new buildings, while agoras—marketplaces—and stoas were characteristic of his new towns. Stoas—lengthy roofed colonnades walled on one side and open on the other—were transplants from Greek towns, where they were places to gather and hold meetings. A stoa lined the temple's Court of Gentiles's inner wall. Incorporating these features in his building sites brought Herod the applause of his hellenized subjects and shrewdly promoted cultural integration to foster social unity and strengthen his kingdom.

In Herod's day Israel was a poor, rocky, and largely arid land with few fertile areas. It extended a mere one hundred and sixty miles north to south and scarcely fifty miles west to east for most of its length, yet this small state paid for Herod's massive building efforts because he undoubtedly supplemented its modest revenues lavishly with his own money.[43]

42. See comment by rabbis cited in Ferguson, *Backgrounds of Early Christianity*, 413.
43. The information on Herod's fiscal apparatus and personal wealth is from Grant,

During his reign's early years, Herod concentrated on consolidating his position in Judea and gaining the emperor's approval. With these objectives largely achieved, by the early twenties he could turn to building up the kingdom. Judea became peaceful and orderly under his skillful administration, while the building program stimulated trade and brought prosperity. He deftly guided Judea in its role as a client state within the Roman Empire, much to the emperor's satisfaction. These mid-reign successes contrast starkly, however, with the troubled atmosphere that enveloped his final years. Uncertainty about the royal succession convulsed his family, and his suspicion-prone personality and mental decline impaired his judgment. Long-suppressed conservative Jewish opposition to him resurfaced, and the imperial goodwill he had tended so carefully withered. He deteriorated physically with a long, painful, and ultimately fatal illness.

As Herod aged the question of his successor loomed ever larger and was complicated by his polygamous marital record. He had at least ten wives and fifteen children, and competition among them for the throne was inevitable. His first choice to succeed him was Alexander and Aristobulus, his two sons by Mariamne, his second wife. This was apparent, for he had sent them to Rome to be educated. On returning to Jerusalem the brothers married wives Herod chose for them: Glaphyra, a pretentious Cappadocian princess, for Alexander; and Berenice, his sister Salome's daughter, for Aristobulus. Friction soon afflicted the royal family, for Glaphyra snobbishly taunted Herod about choosing his wives only for their beauty and ridiculed Berenice's Idumean roots. When vague rumors of the brothers plotting against their father reached Herod through Salome, the tension increased. Suspicious of his sons' intentions, Herod revised his plans for the succession. He recalled Antipater, a long-banished son by his first wife Doris, and named him his successor in what eventually proved to be the first of at least four wills. Since Rome's client kings required the emperor's approval of their prospective successors, and as it was well-known that Herod had intended Alexander and Aristobulus to succeed him, Herod took them to Rome to secure Augustus's consent for his new succession plans. The emperor cleared the brothers of scheming against their father, however, bringing reconciliation between Herod and his sons.

This Augustus-inspired rapprochement proved to be short-lived. On returning to Jerusalem Herod announced that at his death the kingdom would be divided among Alexander, Aristobulus, and Antipater, with the

---

Herod, chapter 11. See also Gabba, "Finances of King Herod," 160–68.

latter being preeminent. While the three feigned acceptance of this arrangement, in reality they were dissatisfied with it. Antipater and his mother sought to discredit Alexander and Aristobulus in Herod's eyes, and soon fresh rumors, possibly true, grew that Alexander was plotting against his father. Terrified of Herod's likely response, Alexander admitted his guilt. When Herod's father-in-law, the Cappadocian king Archelaus, convinced him to accept the confession, the tension eased.[44]

As Herod wrestled with these thorny domestic issues, Judea's relations with the neighboring Nabataeans were worsening. Many years earlier Herod had barred his sister Salome from marrying Syllaeus, the Arab kingdom's chief minister, an insult he never forgot. The aggrieved minister suffered a second rebuff involving Herod when Augustus rejected his request to purchase the territory of Aurantis and gave it to Herod instead. Nabataean-Judean relations declined further in 12, when Syllaeus harbored rebels fleeing from Herod's northern territory of Trachonitis. Matters came to a head shortly after when the Nabataeans failed to repay a loan from Herod; he appealed to Saturninus, Rome's governor in Syria, who gave them thirty days to meet their obligation. When no payment arrived in the allotted time, Herod promptly invaded the Arab territory, setting off the Second Nabataean War. Before returning triumphantly with loot and prisoners, his forces captured a fortress and killed a commander who was Syllaeus's relative.

When word of Herod's attack reached Rome, Syllaeus, who happened to be present, heightened the news's impact by informing Augustus that twenty-five hundred Nabataeans had been killed in the raid. Angered by Herod's rash act—one client king attacking another client king—the emperor severely reprimanded him in a harshly worded letter; in the future Herod, whom he had considered a friend, would be treated as a mere subject. Whether Herod had acted independently or from belief that Saturninus had given his approval is uncertain. In any case, the Nabataean attack was an ill-considered move reflecting Herod's poor judgment, an early sign perhaps of the mental decline that would cast a dark shadow over his final years. It was a serious error that cost him Augustus's confidence, hitherto a vital element in Herod's enviable reputation.

Herod's falling out with the emperor abated somewhat, however, following the death of the elderly Nabataean king Obodas, whom Syllaeus had dominated. Aretas, an enemy of Syllaeus, seized the throne and brashly assumed the title of king before gaining imperial approval. This offended

---

44. Grant, *Herod*, 184–88.

Augustus even more than Herod's Nabataean raid. When Aretas sent envoys to Rome to mollify Augustus, Syllaeus convinced the emperor to ignore them. With Aretas and Herod both out of favor with Augustus, they joined forces to destroy Syllaeus, their common enemy. Nicolaus of Damascus, Herod's capable and eloquent secretary who frequently undertook diplomatic assignments for him, was chosen to carry out this delicate task. Aided by Aretas's agents, he went to Rome in 7 and pressed charges against Syllaeus, claiming that only twenty-five Nabataeans had been slain in Herod's attack, not twenty-five hundred as Syllaeus had reported. Offended at being intentionally misled, Augustus changed his view of the Nabataean-Judean conflict. Syllaeus was sent home to Petra discredited, and ordered to pay Herod the long overdue Nabataean debt. Herod regained imperial favor, but without the full confidence he previously enjoyed. Aretas was admonished for brazenly seizing the throne and claiming the title of king, but was confirmed as king.[45]

As Herod worried about his faltering relations with Augustus and his sons' scheming over the succession, he was further burdened by rising opposition among his subjects. Resistance to him among the Jews had been quiescent since the early twenties, when in response to an assassination plot, as we have seen, he had forthrightly executed the conspirators. It resurfaced in 7 or 6 after he ordered an oath of allegiance to be sworn to the emperor and himself. The Seleucids had used similar pledges, and they were common in the Roman Empire's client kingdoms. Orthodox Jews were sensitive about using God's name with oaths, however, and feared that this might involve worshipping statues of the emperor. Earlier in 17, when Herod had required swearing an oath of allegiance to himself, Essenes and Pharisees had requested exemption from the order, which he granted. The new oath, however, was to Augustus as well as himself, and Herod feared that resisting it might be seen as not merely a discourtesy but outright disloyalty to Rome. The timing strongly suggests that Herod intended it to help restore his flagging status with the emperor. The Essene response is unknown, but when prominent Pharisees refused to comply, he punished them with fines, a surprisingly light penalty given his customary forcefulness in dealing with opponents.

This lenient treatment of the recalcitrant Pharisees in all likelihood was the result of the support for them in his own household, for his brother Pheroras's wife paid their fines. A slave girl whom Pheroras loved dearly,

---

45. Grant, *Herod*, 189-94.

Herod had twice resisted his wish to marry her by proposing prospective wives whom Pheroras rejected. It is little wonder that this woman, whose name is unknown, should back Herod's Pharisee opponents.

Some extremists among this group of Herod's Pharisaic enemies held strong messianic beliefs. They looked for a golden age when through divine intervention a strong king would arise in Judea to redeem God's chosen people, restore their independence, and establish a righteous kingdom on earth. Some even predicted that God would remove the monarchy from Herod's hands and give it to Pheroras, his wife, and their offspring, implying that he was to become the father of the messianic line. Others convinced the eunuch Bogoras, a high official in the royal household, that he would become the father of the messiah-king despite his physical disability. Salome, Herod's conniving sister, gathered this talk through her intelligence network and passed it on to Herod, who disparaged all talk of messianism unless it pointed to him as the chosen one's progenitor. That someone might be scheming to take his place fueled Herod's fears, and he executed Bogoras and his Pharisee supporters. Pheroras also fell under a cloud of suspicion and was forced to remove to Perea, where he soon died. His wife was spared for the moment, but when further inquiries revealed her implication in Herod's son Antipater's plan to assassinate his father, she was executed in 5 BCE. Her death, and the execution of Bogoras and his Pharisaic supporters, further alienated their powerful Pharisee friends. Resistance to Herod now spread, for moderate Jews, who once regarded him as an acceptable alternative to the Hasmoneans whom they hated, also turned against him.

Open resistance erupted the following year. Herod had mounted a gilt eagle over the temple gate, whether recently or during its rebuilding is uncertain, but it was an ideal target for people looking to make trouble for him. Literal interpretation of the Second Commandment's stricture against graven images could readily be applied to animals as well as humans. The eagle was a well-known pagan cultural symbol frequently displayed on Syrian and Roman temples. Two prominent teachers at a Jerusalem Pharisee academy began declaiming in their lectures that Herod's sickness—he was seriously ill by this time—was God's punishment for erecting the eagle in violation of the law. Incited by their accusatory mentors, militant students tore the eagle down, and some forty protestors were promptly arrested by soldiers from the neighboring Antonia Fortress. Brought before Herod for questioning, they boldly declared that they were defending the law. They were tried in Jericho where Herod, so ill that he was carried into the court on his sick bed, gave a bitter diatribe defending his loyal services to the temple in contrast to the Hasmoneans' weak record. He spared most of the demonstrators, but the teachers and the students who destroyed the eagle were burned alive.[46]

Meanwhile in Jerusalem fresh reports surfaced that Alexander and Aristobulus were plotting against Herod, and Antipater, eager to discredit his rival brothers, informed him. Reflecting his deteriorating mental condition, the suspicion-prone Herod began hallucinating about Alexander attacking him with a sword. Convinced that they were planning to kill him, he imprisoned both Alexander and Aristobulus. Lacking the confidence to handle the affair himself, he wrote to Augustus for advice, a surprising step for one known to rule with a firm hand. The emperor, undoubtedly annoyed at being bothered again with the distant Jerusalem court's petty squabbles, curtly told him to punish the brothers if they were guilty of plotting to assassinate him, but merely reprimand them if they had only planned to escape. He advised Herod to resolve the matter by presenting it for settlement to a court outside his jurisdiction. Herod convened a special court at Berytus, a city well-disposed toward him because of his past generosity. Siding with Herod, the Berytus court found the brothers guilty and, disregarding a recommendation of clemency from Nicolaus of Damascus, he had his sons strangled in Sebaste. Whether they had actually conspired to kill their father is uncertain.[47]

The succession issue reverberated well beyond speculation about which of Herod's sons would follow him. Near the end of his reign—the precise date is uncertain, but evidently shortly after Jesus' birth—Herod heard from eastern astrologers that a new king of the Jews had been born. Alarmed, the ever-wary Herod feared that someone other than his choice might succeed him. Learning from priests that the expected Messiah would come from Bethlehem, he ordered all male children up to two years old in the town's region be killed. The heinous directive was unmistakable evidence of Herod's state of mind.[48]

46. On Herod's renewed trouble with the Jews during his reign's late years, see Grant, *Herod*, 204–10, and Grant, *History of Ancient Israel*, 231–33.

47. On the alleged plotting of Alexander and Aristobulus, their trial, and execution, see Grant, *Herod*, 195–99.

48. Matt 2:1–17. Josephus omits any reference to the killing of the Bethlehem children, and some scholars are inclined to treat the story as mythical folklore originating with Herod's later detractors. See Grant, *Herod*, 12; Richardson, *Herod*, 295–97, and

Herod

The execution of Alexander and Aristobulus reduced the tension over Herod's successor that had so disrupted the royal household by increasing the likelihood Antipater would become Herod's heir, but there were still obstacles in his way. Salome, Herod's loyal sister, had incriminating evidence of Antipater's secretive actions that she might reveal. Moreover, Antipater still had at least five half-brothers, and there were signs that they might yet become his rivals for the royal prize, for Herod had taken the trouble to send three of them to Rome to be educated, Archelaus and Antipas, Herod's sons by his Samaritan wife Malthace, and Philip, a son by Cleopatra, his Jewish wife. Nevertheless, Antipater still had good reason to believe that he would attain his goal, for in 5 BCE Herod sent him to Rome bearing a new will naming him the royal heir.

While in Rome, however, disquieting news cast an ominous shadow over his aspirations, for he received word that his mother Doris had been banished from Jerusalem under suspicion. He quickly left Rome for Judea, only to learn more alarming information on route; his ally Pheroras, Herod's brother, had died. Antipater's fate was sealed even before he reached Jerusalem, for during his absence Herod discovered Antipater was plotting to poison him. He was tried before a court presided over by Varus, Rome's governor in Syria, and found guilty.

Having just informed Augustus in his second will that he wanted Antipater to succeed him, Herod wrote the emperor apprising him of the changed circumstances, but before receiving Augustus's reply he named Antipas, his son by Malthace, to be his successor in a third will.[49] With Antipater's unquestioned guilt, and Herod's reputation for resolute behavior, his delay in punishing Antipater is significant. His appeal to Augustus points to his shrinking self-confidence and worsening mental state. This uncharacteristic reluctance to deal forthrightly with Antipater must have further undermined Augustus's confidence in his once-decisive Judean ruler. Roman emperors expected client kings to manage their kingdoms expeditiously, as Herod had done previously; those unable or unwilling to do so were failures in Roman eyes. Augustus's reply acknowledged Antipater's guilt without offering advice on his punishment. With Herod seriously ill, the still-imprisoned Antipater in 4 BCE got word, false as it proved, that Herod had

---

Vermes, *True Herod*, 7, 48.

49. On the naming of Antipater as the royal successor in Herod's second will, his plot to poison Herod, the resulting trial, and Herod's third will, see Grant, *Herod*, 199–203.

died. Determined to seize the throne, he enticed the jailer to free him, but the jailer loyally informed Herod, who ordered his immediate execution.[50]

In severe pain shortly before dying, Herod issued a drastic order directing Judea's leading Jews to gather in Jerusalem on pain of death. On arrival they were incarcerated in the hippodrome, and Salome and her husband were made to promise to kill them with darts immediately following his death. Presumably this was Herod's way of retaliating against the conservative Jewish leadership that had constantly opposed him throughout his reign.[51]

Among his final acts, he wrote a fourth will reverting to the idea of dividing the kingdom, with Archelaus, his son by Malthace, having preeminence. Archelaus would have Judea, Idumea, and Samaria, while Antipas would rule Galilee and Perea. Philip, Herod's son by Cleopatra, was to receive Trachonitas, Batanaea, and Aurantis, areas in the northeast. The coastal towns of Jamnia and Azotus and the interior settlement of Phasaelis were assigned to Salome.[52] These dispersals were Herod's wish for the final division of his kingdom, but it remained to be seen whether Augustus would grant them.

Having reigned thirty-three years, Herod died in the spring of 4 BCE, following a painfully debilitating illness. He was buried south of Jerusalem at Herodium West, his favorite site.

50. Grant, *Herod*, 211–12.
51. Josephus, *Ant.* 17.6.5; 17.6.168–79.
52. Grant, *Herod*, 212.

VIII

After Herod

HEROD'S DEATH LEFT THE kingdom momentarily leaderless, for no successor had been officially sanctioned by the emperor, and three of Herod's sons prepared to defend their respective claims before Augustus. Archelaus, undoubtedly aware that the final will allotted him preeminence in the succession, took charge of Herod's funeral arrangements and quickly assumed leadership, hoping presumably that Augustus would approve. Before he was able to present his case in Rome, however, Jewish nationalists rebelled at Passover in 4 BCE, and in the ensuing violence Archelaus's forces killed some three thousand. A second uprising followed at the feast of Pentecost, with damage to the temple and great loss of life, as roving bands terrorized the countryside threatening anyone supporting Rome. Conditions deteriorated so seriously that Varus, the Roman governor of Syria, intervened with a force of twenty thousand to restore order; numerous towns were destroyed, two thousand rebels were crucified, and upwards of thirty thousand Jews were sold into slavery before he withdrew, leaving a legion in Jerusalem.[1]

In the meantime, Archelaus, Antipas, and Philip appeared in Rome to press their respective claims. Antipas derided Archelaus for seizing power without the emperor's approval and defamed him for the unwarranted slaughter of many Jews during the Passover uprising. The Jews also sent a

---

1. Josephus, *Ant.* 17.9.1–3; 17.10.1–10; Durant, *Caesar and Christ*, 542–43.

delegation to the emperor to voice their complaints. Their deposition bitterly alleged that Herod had long oppressed Judeans and asserted that in view of his recent wanton killing of so many Jews Archelaus intended to continue his father's tyrannical ways. They requested the end of rule by a king and that Judea be attached to Syria with the promise of being allowed to live by their own laws. Nicolaus of Damascus, Herod's former tutor and gifted counselor, refuted both Antipas's and the Jews' charges and eloquently supported Archelaus before Augustus. Nicolaus and Archelaus carried the day, for Augustus acceded to Herod's wishes. Archelaus received Idumea, Judea, and Samaria, to rule with the title of ethnarch (governor) and the possibility of becoming king if he ruled successfully. Antipas and Philip would govern Galilee and Perea, and Trachonitis, Batanaea, and Aurantis, respectively, each with the title of tetrarch (ruler).[2]

Philip ruled his small principality from his capital at Panias, which he rebuilt and named Caesarea Philippi in honor of the emperor. Josephus pictures him as a good ruler who governed quietly. He married Salome, the daughter of Antipas and Herodias, and after ruling thirty-seven years died childless in 34 CE. His tetrarchy was added to Syria.[3]

Antipas (named Herod in Matthew and Mark) ruled Galilee and Perea initially from his capital at Sepphoris and evidently was successful at controlling the troublesome Galileans. Early in his reign he refurbished Betharamphtha, the fortress in Perea, to protect his eastern border from the Nabataeans, and renamed it Julia in honor of Augustus's wife. About 20 he built a new palace on Lake Gennesaret's (Sea of Galilee) western shore and named it Tiberias, after the new emperor. Like Herod, he recognized the importance of accumulating favor with the imperial household, and succeeded in maintaining good relations with Augustus and Tiberius, but he paid dearly for misjudging his standing with Caligula, Tiberius's successor.

It was Antipas's undisciplined personal life that ultimately led to his undoing. He had married the Nabataean king's daughter. Herodias, the ambitious daughter of Antipas's brother Aristobulus, had an "undistinguished" husband who was another brother of Antipas. Seeking to improve her status by becoming the wife of a tetrarch, Herodias inveigled Antipas into divorcing his Nabataean wife and marrying her. This ill-advised union had far-reaching implications. When the prophet John the Baptist, then preaching in Perea, denounced Antipas for marrying Herodias, his brother's wife,

---

2. Josephus, *Ant.* 17.9.4-7; 11.1-5.
3. Josephus, *Ant.* 17.8.1; 18.4.6.

in violation of the law, Antipas imprisoned him. John's denunciation offended Herodias and Salome, her daughter by Antipas, and they schemed to have Antipas execute him.[4] This undoubtedly aroused local opposition, for John had a following. Antipas's divorce of the Nabataean princess also insulted the Nabataean court, and war resulted. When the Nabataeans defeated Antipas in 36, Tiberius had to send the Syrian governor with troops to restore peace.

In the meantime, Agrippa, Herodias's brother and Aristobulus's son, who lived in Rome, had become a friend of Caligula, the future emperor. When Caligula succeeded Tiberius in 37, he gave Agrippa Philip's former tetrarchy, which, as we have seen, had been attached to Syria since Philip's death, and the neighboring principality of Abilene northwest of Damascus, to rule with the title of king. Agrippa's good fortune, however, aroused Herodias's jealousy, and she goaded Antipas to ask Caligula for the title of king as well. This proved to be a crucial mistake. Instead of granting his request, Caligula banished Antipas to Gaul and in 37 gave his tetrarchy to Agrippa, making him king of Galilee and Perea, and Batanaea, Aurantis, and Trachonitis—the combined tetrarchies of Philip and Antipas.[5]

While the reigns of Philip and Antipas were long and moderately successful, turbulence marked Archelaus's ethnarchy. From the outset several conditions over which he had little control encumbered his chance of success. Idumeans and Samaritans were unpopular in Judea, and at best were considered second-class citizens; it was Archelaus's misfortune to be the son of a Samaritan mother and an Idumean father. His domain, much diminished since the days of Herod, meant that its revenues were smaller, and the end of Herod's vast building program brought unemployment. His Roman education predisposed him to continue his father's hellenizing policies, but the Jewish character of his province thwarted this aspiration. As we have seen, violence and insecurity marked his accession to power. It proved to be a harbinger of the future, for the early turmoil continued throughout his entire reign. In desperation a delegation of Jews finally appealed to Augustus to end the kingship. The emperor removed him in 6 CE.[6]

---

4. Matt 14:1-6; Mark 6:14-29.
5. Noth, *History of Israel*, 423-24.
6. Durant, *Caesar and Christ*, 542-43; Grant, *Herod*, 216.

IX

Prefects and Procurators

HEROD'S DEATH AND HIS kingdom's dispersal among his sons mark the Silent Years' end. Seemingly this is the logical place to conclude a survey of the four-hundred-year-gap in the Old Testament account of Israel's history. However, it is less satisfactory than appears at first glance; ending the story here would leave Israel at the peak of its splendor and territorial reach since its grandeur in David and Solomon's time, and the reader wondering about the nation's future. Seventy years later, the First Roman War (66–70) is a more suitable time. Jerusalem is demolished and the temple—the focal point of national life—is destroyed; the sacrificial ritual central to Israel's religious life ends; the office of high priest, whose occupant had been Israel's *de facto* leader since the end of the Babylonian captivity, disappears; and the state of Israel ceases to exist. These events, despite occurring after the Silent Years, warrant an excursus into the first century CE in order to complete the ancient Jews' story. Moreover, it builds a bridge connecting the Old and New Testaments and has the additional benefit of illuminating the context in which the New Testament protagonists functioned and the Christian church was born. The study undertakes this by focusing on the Roman prefects and procurators who governed Israel from Herod's death to the First Roman War.

With Archelaus's banishment Judea became a minor Roman military province, governed by officials initially called prefects, and later procurators, residing at Caesarea Maritima. These figures came from the equestrian order, substantial landowners from the middling ranks in Roman society between the large estate-owning senatorial aristocracy and the third-level common citizens. Ordinarily the prefects were not subject to the Roman governors in Syria, but they might be called on to intervene in unusual circumstances. Relying on locally recruited soldiers garrisoned throughout the province, they handled military affairs and managed provincial finances using taxes raised by Judean tax collectors. The Sanhedrin's traditional functions were preserved, but prefects exercised supreme judicial authority. The death penalty rested in their hands. The Jerusalem religious community was excused from emperor worship, but its members had to take an oath of allegiance to him.[1] Undistinguished for their influence or administrative skill and experience, prefects often served brief terms, affording limited time to learn Judean social customs and religious traditions. This occasionally resulted in misunderstanding and resentment on both sides,[2] but in the main Judea had a satisfactory relationship with Rome for several decades following Archelaus's removal. By midcentury, however, the relationship began to fray, until it ended in the ultimate disaster of the First Roman War. It was in this changing context following Archelaus's removal that the first-century events recounted in the New Testament leading to Christianity's birth occurred.

The first prefect of the newly-erected military province of Judea was Coponius. During his prefecture (6–9 CE), the violence of Archelaus's time threatened to reignite when word spread that Quirinius, the governor of Syria, was about to undertake a census. It raised fear that direct imperial taxation would follow, something Rome had avoided during Herod's reign.[3] Judas, a radical nationalist from Gaulantis, a city east of the Jordan and north of the Yarmuk River, incited talk of rebellion; the census would lead to taxation, he warned, an evil akin to slavery, adding that God would withhold his benevolence if Judeans failed to resist. Joazar, the high priest, wisely counseled the people to ignore Judas's ominous predictions and persuaded them to submit to the census. It was completed peacefully, and the

---

1. Noth, *History of Israel*, 421–22.

2. Grant, *Herod*, 220–21. On Roman social structure in Augustus's time, see Lerner et al., *Western Civilizations*, 166–67. The title "prefect" was changed to "procurator" beginning with Emperor Claudius (41–54); see Ferguson, *Backgrounds of Early Christianity*, 43–44.

3. Richardson, *Herod*, 301. Citing E. Schurer in *History of the Jewish People in the Age of Jesus Christ*, I, 420, Richardson writes "Roman taxes could not possibly have been levied in Palestine" during Herod's reign.

danger of renewed rebellion subsided. Although Judas's call for rebellion failed, the embers of resistance smoldered on below the surface.[4]

From Josephus's account it appears that the three prefectures following Coponius—Marcus Ambivius (9–12), Annius Rufus (12–15), Valerius Gratius (12–26)—were relatively quiet and orderly periods. The atmosphere changed, however, under Pontius Pilate, prefect from 26 to 36, for his low opinion of the Jerusalem religious community and ill-considered actions induced determined Jewish opposition resulting in sharp confrontations.[5]

When troops from Caesarea Maritima moved to winter quarters in Jerusalem, they carried ensigns (flags or banners) bearing the emperor's likeness. This offended the Jerusalem religious community, for their law proscribed images. Moreover, bringing the ensigns into the city was a significant departure from past practice, for previous officials, wary of Jewish reaction, had avoided displaying image-bearing insignia. Whether equipping the soldiers with the ensigns resulted from Pilate's ignorance of Jewish tradition, an underling's careless oversight, or was a calculated move by Pilate to lodge the standards in the city regardless of Jewish custom is uncertain; their nighttime arrival, however, favors the latter explanation. "Multitudes" soon appeared before Pilate in Caesarea Maritima demanding the ensigns be removed. Concerned that withdrawing them might appear dishonoring to the emperor, Pilate refused, and when the supplicants renewed their demand, he sternly warned them to desist. The protestors persisted, however, and Pilate, angered by their perseverance, ordered them to abandon their efforts and return home or face severe consequences for their impertinence. He then signaled soldiers concealed nearby who advanced with drawn weapons. Undeterred, the protestors bravely laid down before him and bared their necks. Moved by their willingness to die rather than see the law violated, Pilate relented; he ordered the offending ensigns returned to Caesarea Maritima, and the crisis passed without violence.[6]

Pilate clashed with Jews a second time over imperial standards when he hung golden shields containing the emperor's name in Herod's former palace in Jerusalem, likely Pilate's residence when visiting the city. The Jews objected because an inscription on them cited Emperor Tiberius's divine paternity, for he was the adopted son of Augustus, whom the Romans

---

4. Josephus, *Ant.* 18.1.1.

5. Noth, *History of Israel*, 422.

6. Josephus, *Ant.* 18.3.1. See also Grant, *History of Ancient Israel*, 236.

deified. The uncompromisingly monotheistic Jews were offended, but evidently abstained from violence over the matter.[7]

A confrontation over Pilate's use of temple funds, however, turned deadly. To increase the city's water supply, Pilate built a twenty-five-mile aqueduct using temple money, seemingly without the council's approval. Large crowds gathered demanding that the project be stopped and during the protest hurled personal insults at Pilate. He responded by sending disguised soldiers with concealed weapons among the crowd. With the insults continuing after he appealed for them to end, he signaled the soldiers to disperse the protesters. Instead, they set upon the crowd, seemingly with more force than Pilate intended. Many bystanders as well as participants were injured and killed before the clash ended.[8]

Despite his willingness to use force against the Judeans, Pilate also accommodated them when it served his interest, as the events leading to Jesus' crucifixion show. Jesus' preaching in Galilee had aroused considerable interest and soon gained the religious leaders' attention, for disquieting rumors began to circulate. Word that he forbade paying taxes and claimed to be king of the Jews—rumors that might arouse the Roman authorities—spread. His denunciation of scribes and Pharisees directly challenged these religious leaders, and his ability to raise a following incited their jealousy, leading some to see him as a potential threat to their leadership. His triumphal appearance in Jerusalem during Passover resulted in a cabal of Jews taking him before the high priest, declaring him guilty of blasphemy and demanding his execution. Without legal authority to impose the death penalty, the Jewish leaders charged him before Pilate with destabilizing Judea by opposing the payment of taxes and claiming to be king of the Jews and the Messiah. Pilate dismissed the accusations, but on learning that he was a Galilean sent him to Antipas, Galilee's tetrarch, then in Jerusalem.

What motivated Pilate is unclear. Given his repeated clashes with the Jews, he may have wanted to avoid the possibility of another incident over an obscure Galilean upstart by having Antipas deal with Jesus. Or the risk of offending Antipas by meddling in a dispute over one of the Galilee tetrarch's subjects may have concerned him. However, Antipas sidestepped being drawn into the affair, for when Jesus declined to answer his questions, he returned him to Pilate mockingly clad in a magnificent robe. After examining Jesus further, Pilate informed the accusers that neither he nor

---

7. Grant, *History of Ancient Israel*, 236–37.
8. Josephus, *Ant.* 18.3.2.

Antipas found any reason to condemn him, and proposed to flog and then release him, but the Jews persisted in calling for his death. After repeatedly affirming Jesus' innocence, but fearful a riot was brewing, he relented and directed Jesus' crucifixion. Pilate had little regard for the Jerusalem religious community's sensitivities, but he was prepared to accommodate its demands, even with an innocent man's death, if it served his interests.[9]

His questionable use of force in Samaria finally brought Pilate's removal. A charlatan convinced a sizable body of Samaritans that he could lead them to a Mount Gerizim site, their holy place, where Moses supposedly had deposited sacred vessels. When the credulous Samaritans gathered to ascend the mountain, Pilate, suspecting the venture's true purpose was rebellion, surrounded them with soldiers, and in the ensuing confrontation some were killed while others fled only to be captured and executed. The Samaritan senate appealed to Vitellus, the Syrian governor, who referred the contretemps to Rome. Pilate was recalled to the imperial capital to answer for his actions, ending his decade-long Judean prefecture.[10]

The two prefects following Pilate—Marcellus (36–37) and Marullius (37–41)—were inconsequential figures, for important matters were in the hands of the Syrian governor Publius Petronius. It was a time of great friction and turmoil resulting from Emperor Caligula's (also called Gaius) egotism. He claimed to be a god and required the emperor to be worshipped throughout the empire. His subjects complied in varying degrees, but the Jews' law prevented them from doing so, and violence soon erupted in Alexandria, where there were many Jews. Flaccus, Roman governor of Egypt, then out of favor with Caligula and anxious to regain his approval, required the emperor's effigy to be placed in Alexandria's synagogues. When the Jews resisted, the city's Greek faction attacked them and destroyed some of their synagogues. In 40 both groups sent delegations to Rome seeking redress from Caligula. The Greek representatives accused the Jews of dishonoring the emperor for opposing his effigy in their synagogues, and when Caligula gave scant heed to the Jewish emissaries' entreaties, strife continued in Alexandria.[11]

Meanwhile the Greeks in Jamnia, a mid-Judean town near the Mediterranean coast, erected an altar for the imperial cult to accommodate Caligula's demand. When the emperor learned that the town's Jews had

---

9. Matt 26:47–68; 27:1–2, 11–31; Mark 14:43–65; 15:1–15; Luke 22:47—23:25.
10. Josephus, *Ant.* 18.4.1–2.
11. Josephus, *Ant.* 18.8.1–2; Noth, *History of Israel*, 425.

destroyed it, he retaliated by ordering Petronius to place a large statue of the emperor in Jerusalem's temple, and threatened war if the Jews resisted. This caused great unrest among the Jews, who appealed to Petronius, claiming they would die before allowing the statue in the temple. Recognizing the danger of a bloody confrontation, Petronius requested the emperor to postpone his order, to no avail. Under mounting pressure from large crowds imploring him to ignore the order, Petronius, risking his life, delayed and again asked Caligula to cancel his directive. Now Caligula's friend Agrippa, to whom the emperor had given Philip's and Antipas's tetrarchies, added his appeal to withdraw the offensive directive. At this critical juncture in early 41, Caligula was assassinated. Claudius, the new emperor (41–54), cancelled the offensive decree, ending the threat of further violence against the Jews and punishment of Petronius for defying Caligula. Claudius also issued an order guarding the Jews' right to practice their religious customs throughout the empire, ending the communal strife in Alexandria.[12]

In the choice of Claudius to succeed Caligula, the Praetorian Guard, the emperor's bodyguards, had been decisive, and Agrippa, then in Rome, had sided with them. Grateful for Agrippa's support, Claudius rewarded him by adding Idumea, Judea, and Samaria, to his kingdom, making Agrippa the client king of virtually the same domain that Herod, his grandfather, had ruled for thirty-three years.[13]

On becoming king in 41, Agrippa assiduously set about cultivating favor with the Jews. He sacrificed in the temple, giving meticulous care to the law's requirements. He gave the temple the golden chain Caligula had given him commemorating his release from prison after his previous injudicious comments about Tiberius. Giving the chain, equal in weight to his iron bonds while in prison, was a dramatic gesture intended to impress the Jerusalem religious community with his piety.[14] He also ended the tax on houses.[15] Mild and even-handed in his personal relations and generous in his gift-giving, Agrippa reveled in the benevolent reputation he acquired. While scrupulously respecting the law in Jerusalem, he readily accommodated Greek customs elsewhere. At Berytus, for example, he built a theater, amphitheater, porticoes, and baths and entertained its residents

---

12. Josephus, *Ant.* 18.8.2–9; 19.5.2–3; Noth, *History of Israel*, 425–26.
13. Josephus, *Ant.* 19.5.1; Noth, *History of Israel*, 425–26.
14. Josephus, *Ant.* 19.6.1.
15. Josephus, *Ant.* 19.6.3.

with bloody gladiatorial shows involving hundreds.[16] His reign, a brief interlude of peace and stability, otherwise was unexceptional and ended abruptly when he died suddenly in 44 at Caesarea Maritima during festive games honoring the emperor.[17]

On Agrippa's death (Agrippa I), Claudius declined to give the kingdom to his son, also named Agrippa (Agrippa II), for he was still an inexperienced teenager. However, in 50 Claudius gave the well-connected Agrippa II, then still living in Rome, the small kingdom of Chalcis located south of Lebanon; his uncle Herod, Agrippa I's brother, had ruled it until his death. Shortly thereafter Chalcis was exchanged for Philip's former tetrarchy and Abilene, a small kingdom northwest of Damascus. This arrangement also gave Agrippa II oversight of the temple and the right to nominate the high priest. Claudius probably saw this as an indirect benefit to the Jerusalem religious community, for to some extent it would insulate temple affairs from interference by Judea's Roman administrators. This authority, which he exercised until the First Roman War's outbreak in 66, enabled Agrippa II to promote the Jerusalem religious community's interests.[18]

With Agrippa I's death Judea reverted to being a Roman province, governed as before by officials now called procurators. Cuspius Fadus (44–46), the first procurator following Agrippa I, caused consternation among Jerusalem's religious leaders by calling for the high priestly vestments to be returned to the Antonia Fortress, where they had been lodged under Herod. Incensed by Fadus's directive, emissaries went to Rome requesting that the sacred paraphernalia be left with the temple authorities. A potentially disruptive issue, it was resolved amicably when Agrippa II, then still in Rome, asked his friend Claudius to grant the request, and the emperor consented. Fadus undoubtedly gained the Judeans' approval for seizing and executing Tholomy, a notorious outlaw, who had victimized numerous Nabataeans and Idumeans.[19]

Although Judea experienced a severe famine under Fadus's successor, Tiberius Alexander (46–48), the danger of it producing social unrest was averted by the Assyrian Queen Helena. A recent Jewish convert, she purchased Egyptian corn and distributed it to the hungry.[20]

---

16. Josephus, *Ant.* 19.7.3–5.
17. Josephus, *Ant.* 19.8.2; Noth, *History of Israel*, 427–28.
18. Josephus, *Ant.* 19.9.2; Noth, *History of Israel*, 433.
19. Josephus, *Ant.* 20.1.1–2.
20. Josephus, *Ant.* 20.5.2; Grant, *History of Ancient Israel*, 239.

Both Fadus and Alexander monitored charlatans and agitators closely, for their numbers were increasing. Thedus, a rogue prophet, gained a following by claiming to be able to part the Jordan's waters. When crowds gathered with their possessions preparing to cross over when he gave the command, Fadus intervened with soldiers to save the prophet's gullible followers from being exploited.[21] Alexander undoubtedly had learned of Judas, the Galilean firebrand who had called for rebellion some thirty years earlier during the Quirinius census, and feared that his two sons James and Simon were following in their father's seditious footsteps. In the atmosphere of the day, when unchecked incendiary talk could stir up trouble leading to armed resistance, Alexander was unwilling to brook their rebellious sentiment, and he crucified them.[22] In general, however, Fadus and Alexander managed relations with the Jews successfully and their era was a peaceful time.[23]

Their successor Ventidius Cummanus, the new procurator (48–52), offered weak leadership, displayed shabby morals, and his term was a time of recurring unrest. Passover was an uneasy time for Roman officials in Jerusalem, for when large numbers gathered for the feast the city was prone to violence. Procurators usually left their Caesarea Maritima headquarters to be in the city in case there was trouble. As a cautionary measure, Cummanus, like his predecessors, stationed soldiers in the cloisters on the temple's periphery during the festival. When a soldier insulted temple visitors by exposing himself to them, some in the enraged crowd charged that Cummanus was behind the incident. The distraught throng refused to disperse after being warned, and Cummanus heightened the tension by moving more soldiers into the adjacent Antonia Fortress. Fearing an imminent attack, the panic-stricken crowd bolted for the temple gates; many were trampled, and Josephus claims thousands perished. That a single soldier's act could cause such a calamity unmistakably reveals Judea's restless state at the time.[24]

With tension still high, some participants in the temple disaster after leaving Jerusalem attacked an imperial official travelling near the city. Incensed by this brazen affront to Roman authority, Cummanus rashly turned soldiers loose on the neighboring towns, with orders to seize their

21. Josephus, *Ant.* 20.5.1.
22. Josephus, *Ant.* 20.5.2.
23. Noth, *History of Israel*, 434.
24. Josephus, *Ant.* 20.5.3.

leaders. During this ill-conceived response, a soldier publicly mutilated a copy of the law presumably taken from a local synagogue. When word of this spread, a large contingent of Jews went to Caesarea Maritima and called on Cummanus to requite their sacred writing's desecration. Fearing the incident might incite an uprising if left unavenged, the worried procurator beheaded the offending soldier, and the danger subsided.[25]

Cummanus's incompetence exacerbated the unrest simmering in Judea by exploiting a hostility-inducing incident between Galileans and Samaritans for his personal gain rather than acting promptly to resolve it. Galileans attending Jerusalem festivals usually travelled through Samaria. When Samaritans attacked a group of them on their way to Jerusalem, killing many, Galilean leaders called on Cummanus for redress, but he ignored their request after being bribed by Samaritans. Vexed at Cummanus's inaction, Galilean zealots, joined by Jewish rebels and Eleazar's bandits, a notorious gang of regional outlaws, took matters into their own hands and sacked a number of Samaritan villages. Warned by alarmed Jewish leaders that this could endanger the entire Jerusalem religious community, Cummanus imprisoned some of the miscreants and executed others.

Seeking retribution for their ravaged towns and despairing of further action by Cummanus, the Samaritans took their cause to Ummidus Quadratus, the Syrian governor, while the Jerusalem religious community threw its support to the Galileans. With the case before Quadratus, the Samaritans charged the Jews with burning their towns, and the Jews countered by blaming the Samaritans for starting the trouble with their attack on the Jerusalem-bound Galileans and boldly accused Cummanus of accepting Samaritan bribes. Quadratus resolved the matter by sending those involved—the Samaritans, the high priest, and Cummanus—to Rome to answer for their actions before Claudius. Initially the emperor was inclined to blame the Jews, but Agrippa II, still in Rome, exploited his friendship with Agrippina, the emperor's wife, and Claudius changed his mind. The Jews were exonerated, the Samaritans were found guilty and executed, and the corrupt and ineffectual procurator Cummanus was banished in disgrace.[26]

Conditions in Judea worsened markedly under Cummanus's successor, Antonius Felix (52–60). Although a favorite of the emperor, he soon made himself hated in Judea.[27] Having three wives, one with whom he had

---

25. Josephus, *Ant.* 20.5.4.
26. Josephus, *Ant.* 20.6.1–3; Noth, *History of Israel*, 434.
27. Noth, *History of Israel*, 434.

a scandalous relationship before she divorced her husband, Felix's personal life offended the Jews. Imposters and charlatans became so numerous that seizing them was a daily occurrence; he punished them ruthlessly, along with their misguided followers. When an Egyptian rogue lured his credulous supporters to the Mount of Olives promising to miraculously destroy Jerusalem's walls, soldiers were unleashed on them and four hundred perished. Felix's treachery was revealed by his troubled relations with Jonathan, an honorable high priest. Indignant over Jonathan's continued stream of unwanted advice for improving relations with the Jews, Felix arranged Jonathan's murder in the temple by paid killers posing as worshippers; then the assassins turned to killing their enemies with equal impunity. Insecurity spread as roving bands of radicals called for rebellion against Rome and attacked those who opposed them, while the sicarii, daggermen with concealed weapons, murdered randomly throughout the countryside and preyed on unsuspecting crowds during festivals in Jerusalem.[28]

Unrest also infected cities. Jerusalem became troubled after Agrippa II appointed Ismael to be high priest. It was a controversial appointment that raised sharp conflict between the chief priests and popular city leaders, each backed by supporting groups. Their verbal confrontations grew into periodic street battles, and Jerusalem turned into a city lacking civic authority, yet Felix seemingly did little to control the disorder.[29]

Turmoil erupted in Caesarea Maritima when Samaritans, claiming superior status, attempted to restrict the rights of Jews. The Jews insisted on their right to equal treatment, because Herod, a Jew by birth, if not heritage, had built the city. The Samaritans denied their claim, arguing that before Herod's building program made it a great port Caesarea Maritima had been the site of Strato's Tower, where no Jews lived. City authorities contained the dispute for a time, but when it turned violent, with the Jews prevailing, Felix, who had left the matter in local hands, intervened and ordered the Jews to desist. When they persisted, he attacked them with force. Many were arrested and killed, and the soldiers freely plundered the wealthy Jewish leaders' houses until moderate Jews persuaded Felix to restrain them.[30]

While Felix was procurator the apostle Paul came under his immediate jurisdiction as a prisoner, following a dangerous confrontation with Asian Jews in Jerusalem. When Paul was interrogated before the council a

28. Josephus, *Ant.* 20.8.5–6.
29. Josephus, *Ant.* 20.8.8.
30. Josephus, *Ant.* 20.8.7.

volatile dispute erupted between Pharisees and Sadducees (as we shall see in the following chapter), resulting in his case being referred to Felix. He questioned Paul repeatedly, but the case remained unresolved when Felix was recalled to Rome two years later.

Felix's failure to resolve the issue of the Caesarea Maritima Jews' rights assured that it was still a hotly contested issue when Porcius Festus (60–62) replaced him as procurator. A delegation of the city's Jews to Rome urged protection of their rights and accused Felix for his violent assault on them. Josephus believes that they would have succeeded if the emperor Nero's brother had not intervened on Felix's behalf. Through the machinations of a Greek delegation Nero was convinced to issue an edict denying Jews their customary rights in Caesarea Maritima. This intensified their discontent and they became "more disorderly than before."[31] Robbery was prevalent throughout Judea, where villages were being burned, and the treacherous sicarii infested Jerusalem's festivals. This disorderly state of affairs greeted Festus, a "fair and just man," when he arrived in Judea. Festus summoned Paul soon after his arrival to appear before him to answer the charges of his Jewish opponents. In his defense he denied offending against Jewish law, the temple, or the emperor and appealed to have his case tried by the emperor's tribunal. Festus consented and sent him to Rome. But Festus succeeded in doing little to improve Judea's chaotic conditions during his brief two-year term, for he died unexpectedly.[32]

Luceius Albinus (60–64) succeeded Festus. In the interim before the new procurator arrived, the high priest Ananus, a brash figure seemingly eager to exert his authority, assumed control and took a step that worried Jerusalem's moderate Jews. He tried James, the brother of Jesus, before the Sanhedrin; it found him guilty of violating the law, and he was stoned. This was a reckless act, for in Judea only Roman officials could impose the death penalty. The moderate Jews, fearing that the procurator would retaliate for Ananus's unwarranted action, appealed to Agrippa II to restrain Ananus and sent a delegation to meet Albinus then on his way to Judea. Apprised of Ananus's injudicious action, Albinus warned him in an angry letter that he would be punished. In the meantime, Agrippa II removed him from the office of high priest. Albinus assumed power in Judea at a critical time — just as Caesarea Maritima Jews were about to learn that the emperor would not protect their traditional rights, and when Ananus's high-handed move

31. Josephus, *Ant.* 20.8.9.
32. Noth, *History of Israel*, 434.

was inviting harsh measures by the procurator and causing sharp division among Jerusalem Jews.

These were troubling conditions requiring careful handling, but Albinus was an abject failure and used his office for personal gain. Josephus writes there was no "wickedness that could be named but that he had a hand in it."[33] Initially he tried to calm the troubled waters by striking at the sicarii, but then unwisely burdened the Judeans with heavy taxation. His shameless corruption was evident in his dealing with Ananias. The wealthy former high priest, who had welcomed and befriended him with a shower of gifts, callously sent his servants into the countryside to seize the threshing floor tithes that rightly belonged to the lesser priests. Ananias's generosity seemingly bought Albinus's complicity, for the offenders went unpunished. Others joined in the pillaging, and numerous priests, deprived of their accustomed income, languished in poverty or perished.[34]

Meanwhile the sicarii, considerable numbers of whom Albinus had imprisoned, used bold tactics to gain their fellow sicarii's release. They seized a temple scribe, a son of Ananias, and offered to free him for the release of ten sicarii prisoners. When Albinus consented, the sicarii resorted to this outrageous tactic repeatedly, brazenly seizing servants of the high priest and exchanging them for sicarii prisoners. Many sicarii detainees were freed, their ranks were replenished, and they continued victimizing Judeans with Albinus's collusion.[35]

On learning he was soon to be replaced, Albinus anticipated that trouble might await him in Rome. Knowing undoubtedly that his predecessor Felix had been accused before Nero for his violent treatment of the Caesarea Maritima Jews, and hoping to avoid a similar fate, he implemented a lamentable plan intended to improve his standing with Judeans. He carried out a mass execution of prisoners in Judean jails guilty of serious crimes, but permitted relatives of lesser offenders to pay him for their release. Many convicts were freed, and Albinus profited handsomely.[36]

Judean resistance to Rome had simmered ever since Archelaus's removal at the beginning of the century. Judas, the Galilean rebel, had warned Judeans against Quirinius's census, as we have seen, claiming that taxation would enslave them, and he urged them to resist. While the high

33. Josephus, *Wars* 2.14.1.
34. Noth, *History of Israel*, 434; Josephus, *Wars* 2.14.1; Josephus, *Ant.* 20.9.2.
35. Josephus, *Ant.* 29.9.3.
36. Josephus, *Ant.* 20.9.5; Josephus, *Wars* 2.14.1.

priest's counsel of moderation prevailed and nothing came of Judas's effort, the Zealots, as his followers became known, continued their hostility. They refused to pay taxes to a foreign power and advocated using armed force to free Judea. Devoted like the Pharisees to the worship of the one God, and sharing their respect for the law, they nevertheless despised the Pharisees for weakly submitting to rule by a foreign power as a necessary evil. The Sadducees were even worse in their eyes, for they were content to live under the Romans. The Zealots incited no major uprisings during the first third of the century and the vast majority of Judeans probably paid them little attention. However, the Zealots were behind numerous lesser incidents, thereby contributing to the ubiquitous sense of unrest that pervaded Judea. In 40, a time of rising tension in Judea, as we have seen, Emperor Caligula's peremptory order that his statue be placed in the temple might have brought rebellion. It was averted by Syrian governor Petronius's delaying tactics in implementing the imperial directive. And Judean king Agrippa I (41–44), Prefect Marulla's successor, preserved the peace by his solicitude for the Jerusalem religious community's interests.

Deterioration marked the following decades, however, as men with limited administrative experience, skill, and a propensity for extracting personal gain from their position filled the procuratorial office. The climax came with Albinus's departure, when Gessius Florus (64–66) became procurator. Josephus describes him as being so corrupt that it made Albinus seem like Judea's "benefactor."[37] He "plundered the land quite openly and without restraint," writes Martin Noth, "and whenever there was a chance of deriving personal advantage from it he gave full scope to disorder and robbery."[38]

Tension mounted ominously in 66, when the Caesarea Maritima Jews, having abandoned hope of securing their traditional rights after Nero rejected their claims, withdrew to Narbata several miles to the east. Open rebellion soon followed when Florus, claiming the emperor needed funds, removed seventeen talents from the temple treasury. An angry crowd mocked him by circulating a basket to collect money for the supposedly needy procurator. Stung by this caustic protest, Florus allowed soldiers to brutally plunder a section of the city with much loss of life and then ordered Jerusalem to prepare a ceremonial welcome for two cohorts of soldiers he dispatched from Caesarea Maritima. Voicing the sentiments of Jerusalem's moderates, and hoping to preserve peace, the high priest

---

37. Josephus, *Ant.* 20.11.1.
38. Josephus, *Ant.* 20.11.1; Noth, *History of Israel*, 435.

implored the people to comply. When the arriving soldiers failed to fittingly acknowledge Jerusalem's formal reception, crowds vented their contempt by verbally abusing Florus, and the troops responded with force. Occupying the temple, the enraged crowd destroyed the portico adjoining the Antonia Fortress to prevent its soldiers from attacking. Without a force large enough to control the situation, Florus withdrew to Caesarea Maritima, leaving a single cohort of troops. Agrippa arrived at this juncture and publicly urged Jerusalemites to cease resisting, but the population was no longer willing to obey Florus, and Agrippa left in failure.[39]

With radical support growing among Jerusalem's contending factions, daily sacrifices on behalf of the emperor long offered in the temple were discontinued, a step signaling a complete break with Rome. Backed by the moderate-minded Pharisee leaders, the high priest desperately sought to quell the roiling chaos by calling on Agrippa to bring a force to Jerusalem and restore order. After a long and bitter struggle in the temple area, his soldiers retreated to Herod's palace, but eventually withdrew in failure, and the committed rebels occupied the Antonia Fortress. They promised the greatly-outnumbered Roman cohort safe egress from Herod's palace, but treacherously slaughtered them as they withdrew. The high priest was murdered and his palace burned, along with the old Hasmonean palace and a portion of Herod's palace.[40]

When it was clear that Florus had lost control in the province, in the fall of 66 Cestius Gallus, governor of Syria, intervened to suppress the nascent rebellion. He came south with a force, occupied a northern suburb of Jerusalem, and launched an attack on the temple. The effort failed, however, and, realizing that his force was too weak to overcome the determined insurgents defending Jerusalem, he retreated to Antioch.[41]

Although radicals were increasing in Jerusalem and throughout the province, they faced significant obstacles in their cause. They lacked military experience and war materiel and were hampered by divisions among themselves, not to mention the lack of cohesion in Judea's heterogenous population. To prepare for the inevitable Roman attack, they divided the province into sectors and placed each under a commander. Galilee, with its relatively compact population and allegiance to the Jerusalem religious community,

---

39. Josephus, *Wars* 2.14.5–6, 9; Noth, *History of Israel*, 436.

40. Noth, *History of Israel*, 437. For an account of the events from the outbreak of war in 66 to the fall of Jerusalem in 70, see Goodman, *Rome and Jerusalem*, 11–29.

41. Noth, *History of Israel*, 437.

was especially important strategically, for Roman forces were likely to strike there first. To prepare the region, Josephus (the future historian), a member of Jerusalem's moderate Pharisee stock that opposed carrying resistance to the extreme and probably hoped for reconciliation with Rome, was appointed its military commander. He was wary of the Galilee Zealots headquartered in the area's northern region at Gischala and their leader John. Josephus's moderation made him a traitor in their eyes, but their effort to assassinate him failed. He formed a sizable Galilean army, but recognizing that its lack of training and experience would limit its effectiveness against disciplined Roman soldiers, he fortified several regional cities.[42]

Following Gallus's failure to subdue the rebellion, Emperor Nero sent Vespasian, a veteran Roman general, to stamp out the uprising. In the winter of 66–67 he and his son Titus marshaled forces at Ptolemais and in the spring advanced on Galilee. When Vespasian's soldiers appeared many of Josephus's forces fled into the fortifies cities, and the countryside was quickly subdued. The remainder of Josephus's troops gathered in Jotapata, but after a forty-seven-day siege the city fell. Josephus escaped, but soon surrendered to Vespasian, who treated him leniently. When John of Gischala fled from Jotapata, Titus seized it with little resistance. By late 67 Vespasian controlled all Galilee and put his army into winter quarters at Caesarea Maritima and Scythopolis.[43]

Galilee's fall quickly resonated in Jerusalem, for after escaping from Titus the Gischala Zealots fled to the city, where they soon clashed with the moderate Sanhedrin. When the Zealots occupied the temple precinct, the city's inhabitants recoiled at the prospect of placing themselves in these turbulent extremists' hands. Needing assistance, the Zealots turned to the Idumeans and with their help overwhelmed their Jerusalem opponents and gained mastery of the city. Offended by this unexpected outcome, and concluding that their aid had been requested under false pretenses, the Idumeans withdrew. By this time radicals had also overcome moderates in many outlying areas of the province. It was likely at this point that the Christian community left Jerusalem for Pella in the Decapolis on the central Jordan Valley's eastern side, an area outside the region impacted by the rebellion.[44]

---

42. Noth, *History of Israel*, 438.
43. Noth, *History of Israel*, 439–40.
44. Noth, *History of Israel*, 440.

In the spring of 68 Vespasian led his army south from Caesarea Maritima toward the Judean heartland. After subduing Idumea and Samaria, he occupied Jericho and prepared to attack Jerusalem. At this point events in Rome disrupted his Palestine campaign, for in June word came of Nero's death. With no head at the apex of the imperial power structure, Vespasian halted his campaign until the question of Nero's successor was resolved. Since there was no established procedure for replacing an emperor, Nero's death potentially could have serious repercussions throughout the empire. Competition for the office among aspiring figures meant that governors in outlying regions had to choose carefully whom to favor in the contest, for backing a loser could have grave consequences. Vespasian wisely suspended his war against the rebels in mid-68, as he was about to lay siege to Jerusalem, until the situation in Rome had stabilized.[45]

Vespasian could afford to delay his attack on Jerusalem without fear of endangering his success, for those holding the city were weakened by violent internecine strife. A gang led by Simon bar Giora had pillaged throughout the countryside unoccupied by the Romans. Simon then moved against Jerusalem's occupants, intending to control the city himself. The Jerusalemites, resisting John of Gischala's tyrannical rule, opened the gates to Simon's band. John and the Zealots withdrew to the temple, and Simon bar Giora and his force ruled the rest of Jerusalem from the spring of 69. A three-way division existed among the occupants of Jerusalem as it awaited the Roman attack in 69: the moderates scattered throughout the city, the Zealots under John of Gischala encamped in the temple complex, and Simon bar Giora's forces that dominated the area beyond the temple.[46]

During the lull in the war, three different figures briefly held the emperorship in Rome, and the last one was murdered in December of 69. In the interval, support for Vespasian was growing in the east. In July 69 he was declared emperor in Egypt, and shortly thereafter in Palestine and Syria, and then throughout the entire eastern part of the empire. In the summer of 70 he left for Rome to resolve the emperorship question, leaving Titus to complete the Judean campaign.[47]

Titus's preparations to attack Jerusalem in the spring of 70 forced the city's factions to combine their defensive efforts. He invited them to surrender, and laid siege when they refused. The temple burned in August and

---

45. Noth, *History of Israel*, 440.
46. Noth, *History of Israel*, 440–41.
47. Noth, *History of Israel*, 441.

Since Babylon

resistance finally collapsed in September. The victors murdered and plundered throughout the city, which suffered devastating destruction. John of Gischala and Simon bar Giora were captured, and with other specially chosen rebel leaders they were marched through Rome in Titus's triumph in 71.

Jerusalem's fall marked the end of the rebellion, but three strongholds—Herodium, Machaeras, and Masada—remained in rebel hands. Herodium surrendered without a fight, and Machaeras's defenders submitted after a siege, but taking Masada was much more problematic because of its nearly impregnable location on a high promontory on the western shore of the Dead Sea. The task fell to Flavius Silva, the procurator 73–81. He circumvallated the entire site with a wall and built a rampart to support his army's siege engines. The remains of these installations and his army's encampment are still evident. The siege ended in 74, when, after a heroic stand, the defenders committed suicide *en masse*. Only two women and five children survived.[48]

Jerusalem's religious community was decimated by the city's fall. With the temple's destruction, which there was no chance of rebuilding, the ancient sacrificial system ended, the office of high priest disappeared, and the Sanhedrin ceased to exist. Synagogue worship, which had existed for many years, replaced the temple's function in Jewish culture. Leadership of the religious community, previously exercised by the priestly aristocracy through the high priest, the temple establishment, and the Sanhedrin fell to the Pharisees. They gathered the remnants of the Jerusalem religious community at Jamnia near Judea's Mediterranean coast. There they formed the Supreme Council consisting of seventy-two "elders," who were mostly Pharisaic scribes. It was responsible for authoritative interpretation and application of the law. Procurators continued to exercise Roman power in Judea; they largely left the council of elders alone, and the council sought to avoid encroaching on Roman judicial authority. The council's reputation grew, and gradually its decisions were accepted throughout the diaspora. Its chairman became known as the "ruler," and he enjoyed great prestige. This began the learned Rabbinic tradition, which a number of famous and influential men like Jochanan bar Zakkai and Gameliel II represented over time.[49]

---

48. Noth, *History of Israel*, 442–45.
49. Noth, *History of Israel*, 445–46.

X

Reprise and Finale

THE JUDEANS' RETURN FROM Babylonian captivity had been and still is regarded as a momentous event in Israel's history. Persian help had enabled them to reoccupy Jerusalem, rebuild the temple, and rekindle a sense of national identity. They recovered elements of their traditional religious practices abandoned during the exile and formally renewed their allegiance to the law. The books of Ezra and Nehemiah recount this process in some detail, but the reader's curiosity about the ensuing years in Israel's history is not satisfied. The biblical narrative ends abruptly with no explanation, leaving one to wonder about Israel's journey through the succeeding four centuries—the Silent Years of the Old Testament canon.

Ruled by governors appointed from their own ranks by Persian monarchs, the Judeans had existed for two centuries as a sub-region of the Persian Empire's Province Beyond the River. Alexander's late-fourth-century defeat of the Persians changed little for the Judeans, for he confirmed their right to practice traditional religious customs. His short-lived empire broke apart early in the third century, and several hellenized regional monarchies replaced it. Two of them, the Ptolemaic and the Seleucid, repeatedly fought each other for control of Palestine, but their wars caused minimal disruption in Judea. The Egyptian-based Ptolemies prevailed initially, and their rule brought relatively stable conditions for their Judean wards during the third century. This stability continued for several decades, until the Syrian Seleucids defeated the Ptolemies at the beginning of the second century.

The stability deteriorated rapidly during the midcentury. Following Alexander's defeat of the Persians, some Jews welcomed Hellenism's pervasive penetration of their region as a progressive force, but others feared its corrosive impact on their traditional ways. These opposing views were dividing Judean society by that period. Contemporaneously, their Seleucid overlords were under pressure from the expanding Roman Empire in the north and the restive Parthians in the east. Seeking to parry these forces by reenforcing his domain's cultural unity, Antiochus IV resorted to banning Israel's customary religious practices and replaced them with new rituals. This intensified the cleavage among Judeans; hellenized Jews were prepared to abandon their traditional rites, but conservative Jews resisted forcefully. The Maccabean rebellion resulted.

The Maccabean rebellion began as a religious movement intent on defending Israel's religious practices, but its objective changed. When Antiochus rescinded his odious decrees, conservative Jews withdrew their support, but the rebel leaders opted to continue the uprising in pursuit of Judean independence. Skillfully exploiting the ongoing conflicts among rival aspirants to the Seleucid throne, they successfully reclaimed Israel's virtual independence about 140 BCE.

The combination of religious and nationalistic motives which energized the early Hasmoneans faded rapidly in the dynasty's middle years. Initially Hyrcanus (134–04) concentrated on defending Judea's newly-won independence, but he adopted an expansionist foreign policy following Antiochus VII's death; he annexed Idumea and extended Judean rule into Samaria and beyond the Jordan. The later Hasmonean years were singularly dissolute. Aristobulus (104–03) murdered his brother and starved his mother in order to win power, before subduing the Itureans in northern Galilee. Alexander Jannaeus (103–76) added more territory to the national domain, but his opulent secularity, personal degeneracy, and hellenized court offended many and exhausted his domestic support. Crucifying hundreds of rebellious men and killing their wives and children before their eyes as he frolicked with his courtesans characterized the cruelty and terror he used to maintain his power. Ironically the later Hasmonean dynasty's corruption and brutality resembled the Hellenizing regime the Maccabees had overthrown to preserve their religious traditions and regain independence eighty years earlier.

By Alexandra Salome's time (76–67) the Hasmonean dynasty already was in serious decline. It lacked a firm base of support in a society riven by division among the aristocratic landowning Sadducees, the conservative Pharisees, and reclusive groups like the Essenes. Moreover, it failed to build a resilient self-sustaining political structure and, like most ancient regimes, lacked an orderly mode of conveying political authority to successive leaders. When Salome died leaving no strong successor, the ensuing Hyrcanus-Aristobulus struggle for the throne further weakened a dynasty devitalized by corruption and increasingly dependent on force to sustain itself.

The Hasmoneans gained independence and preserved traditional Jewish religious forms after centuries of enthrallment to foreign powers, but during their eight-decade reign they gradually adopted the ways of neighboring hellenized kingdoms. Weakened by corruption and relying on naked force to sustain themselves, they became alienated from their subjects under Alexander Jannaeus. But even if the later Hasmoneans had been led by wise and creative leaders, there was virtually no possibility they could have maintained Judean independence, for by the mid-first-century BCE Rome had become dominant in the eastern Mediterranean.

Pompey's seizure of Judea in 63 ended eighty years of Judean independence. He reconfigured the Seleucid Empire as the Roman province of Syria and reduced the Hasmonean kingdom to a Roman dependency about the size of the old province of Judea. Julius Caesar, emperor after defeating Pompey in 48, named Hyrcanus ethnarch of Judea and made his Idumean chief minister Antipater Judean procurator with Roman citizenship. This enabled Antipater to appoint his son Herod *strategos* of Galilee, opening the door to his brilliant future.

The gifted and ambitious young Herod rose to political power in Judea within a decade, his despised Idumean roots notwithstanding. He overcame the Jerusalem council's challenge to his gubernatorial authority and astutely married into Hasmonean royalty. With Mark Antony and Octavian's support, he convinced the Roman senate to appoint him king of Judea. Bolstered by imperial aid, he ousted the Parthians' puppet king from Jerusalem, and by 37 BCE was in possession of the city and the throne of Judea.

Known to many only from his brief appearance in the New Testament as the wicked ruler who ordered Bethlehem's male children slaughtered, in reality Herod was one of Israel's great kings, with a remarkable record of achievement. In conditions demanding astute judgment and adroit maneuvering, he became a strong ruler who skillfully administered his kingdom for most of his thirty-three-year reign. As a client king he was responsible for collecting the annual tribute and providing men and war materiel when the Roman Empire requested it, but otherwise he was free to manage his domestic affairs. When he seized their land and executed the Sadducee aristocrats who resisted his entry into Jerusalem, it was clear from the outset that he would crush opposition and rule with a firm hand. Unlike Alexander Jannaeus, however, he didn't sustain his regime with brute force and was a prudent fiscal manager who avoided burdening his kingdom with debt.

As a clear-sighted realist, Herod understood that Judea had no hope of regaining independence when Rome was the undisputed master of the Mediterranean world. Recognizing that Judea's wellbeing depended on alignment with Rome, he wisely shaped his policies accordingly. Although the ruler of a client kingdom, his administrative dexterity kept imperial officials away and retained control of provincial affairs in local hands. Unstable during the troubled years following Salome's death, Judea became peaceful and orderly under his guidance.

Herod faced the challenge of establishing priorities among the various forces competing for his allegiance: his Idumean heritage, his respect for Hellenism, his Jewish religion, and the necessity of aligning Judea's interest with the Roman Empire's. Forced to choose among these competing loyalties, a weaker leader might have vacillated and ultimately lapsed into fatal inactivity. Instead, Herod traversed this formidable politico-cultural terrain with surefooted skill, for an unwavering commitment to Judea's well-being, balanced by the necessity of accommodating Rome, anchored his decision-making. As Judean king, this was his primary obligation, a responsibility he lost sight of only in his last days.

Although he ruled a Jewish kingdom, Herod never felt fully Jewish, and he failed to win the full confidence of the nationalists and radicals among his subjects. His willingness to accommodate Rome and his affection for Hellenism offended them. To some he was the instrument of divine punishment for Judea's unfaithfulness which they must endure. Others accepted him begrudgingly as a preferable alternative to his hedonistic Hasmonean predecessors. After dramatically showing he would not brook open resistance by executing participants in a suspected assassination plot in the early twenties, he forged a practical understanding with his detractors; this mutual accommodation survived until the latter stages of his reign.

His reign is celebrated for its great building efforts, remnants of which still exist. Their variety and advanced technology continue to attract architects' wonder and study. The buildings reflect his attraction to Hellenistic culture, while the temple, the crowning achievement of his building projects, reveals his respect for Jewish tradition. The massive expenditure they required fostered economic growth, enriched merchants with expanded trade, secured workers abundant opportunities for employment, and brought ordinary Judeans prosperity they had never known.

When a two-year drought devastated the region's food supply inflicting great suffering on Judeans, Herod responded compassionately. He used money from the sale of his own valuables to import Egyptian grain and supply the sick and elderly with bread. When drought decimated their sheep and goat herds, depriving them of wool for weaving, the destitute received clothing to see them through the winter. Even the Syrians were sent seeds.[1] At the drought's end, he supplied a large workforce to help with the harvest and returned a third of the taxes.[2] With substantial contributions from his personal wealth, he underwrote the prodigious building program that enriched Judea's cultural life and stimulated its economy.

Herod's reign, nevertheless, was an enigmatic one, exhibiting a combination of clear-sighted realism, deft administration, and public-spirited generosity on one hand and suspicion-driven cruelty on the other. The constructive forces dominated much of his career, but the dark energies embedded in his complicated personality surfaced on occasion, rendering him capable of using brutal force against those who blocked his way or whom he suspected were plotting against him. On gaining power he summarily executed forty-five Sadducees who had resisted his entry into Jerusalem, virtually wiping out Judea's land-owning aristocracy—the same group that had threatened him a decade earlier over his actions in Galilee. Even family members were vulnerable when his suspicion was aroused. He executed his second wife Mariamne, his mother-in-law Alexandra II along with her eighty-year-old father who was the former high priest Hyrcanus, a teenage brother-in-law, two adult brothers-in-law, and three of his sons. There is ample reason for seeing Herod as a cruel, paranoid monarch with an abominable record of killing.

Herod's behavior, however, must also be viewed in the context of his time. His world had yet to solve the problem of peacefully passing power to successive leaders. This induced worry and suspicion on the part of aging rulers, as their prospective political successors schemed endlessly about the future—intrigue and cruelty were endemic in Hellenistic courts.

1. Josephus, *Ant.* 15.9.1–2; Grant, *Herod*, 122–23.
2. Josephus, *Ant.* 15.10.4; 16.2.4; Vermes, *True Herod*, 68.

Since Babylon

Michael Grant cautions against allowing the monstrous events of Herod's late reign to unduly color one's overall assessment of his monarchy. As long as his judgment was unimpaired, Grant writes, Herod "achieved as much greatness as was possible for any man of his time who was not Roman. He devoted his many talents to making Judea as peaceful, important, and prosperous a country as it was capable of becoming in a world dominated by the western power [Rome]."[3] In his final years, however, the stress of balancing Judea's wellbeing against the necessity of accommodating Rome, the burden of continuous family turmoil, the resurgence of Jewish opposition, and his painful and fatally debilitating illness combined to overwhelm the mental power that had sustained him throughout his reign. His faltering judgment cost him Augustus's confidence, the bedrock of his previous success. The unnecessary oaths of allegiance he demanded rekindled Jewish opposition. He enflamed the situation further by erecting the eagle over the temple gate, which ignited student protest with its barbarous outcome. Only a seriously disordered mind could have initiated more family murders, to say nothing of the Bethlehem infant slaughter, and the arrangements for killing Judea's leading Jews on word of his death.

The Silent Years, the mystifying four-century gap in the Old Testament narrative of Israel's history, end with Herod's long and controversial reign. For most of that time the Jewish state had been a dependency of neighboring powers. Yet, except for a brief period under Antiochus Epiphanes which led to the Maccabean rebellion and eighty years of independence, the Jews seemingly were not oppressed by their overlords. In fact, as a client kingdom of Rome, they experienced a remarkable measure of prosperous autonomy; as long as the annual tribute was paid and men and materiel were supplied when Rome requested them, Herod was free to govern as he saw fit. Shielded by the *Pax Romana* and guided by Herod's administrative dexterity, Judea became peaceful and orderly. It benefited from the prosperity his vast building program fostered, and expanded virtually to its original size in the days of the united kingdom. However, the Judean court strayed far from its ancestors' commitment to live by the law under Ezra and Nehemiah, and Herod's erratic behavior in his final years obscures his astonishing achievements. Barring his mental collapse and the exhaustion and debilitating illness that distorted his judgment, his kingdom's reputation would rival the reigns of David and Solomon in historical memory.

---

3. Grant, *Herod*, 231.

Reprise and Finale

Herod's death marked not only the end of the Silent Years, it was a major turning point in ancient Israel's later history, occurring at the height of Israel's splendor and wealth. Because there was no designated successor with skill and vision to replace him, the kingdom was divided among his three sons. Antipas and Philip were adequate rulers of their respective territories, but Archelaus, who received Judea, Idumea, and Samaria—Israel's heartland—only survived for a decade before being removed. His holding became a minor Roman province to which Antipas and Philip's territories were added by 40 CE. The orderly future promised by the quality of Agrippa I's brief reign in the early forties failed to materialize because of his untimely death. Led by incompetent and corrupt Roman governors after midcentury, Judea descended into disorder and violence, ending with Israel's disappearance in the First Roman War. Had the kingdom remained intact with a ruler even marginally resembling Herod, Israel might have continued as the client kingdom it was in Herod's day.

Herod's brief mention in the New Testament, the source of most people's knowledge of him, ensures that he is commonly known only as the barbarous ruler responsible for the Bethlehem infant massacre.[4] His place in Israel's history is as ambiguous and little-known to Christian laity as the climax of the Jews' history during the Silent Years. The historical window on the Silent Years closes leaving the curious-minded more knowledgeable about Israel's experience during the four hundred years following the return from Babylon, but still wondering why the Old Testament canon omits this significant epoch in the history of God's chosen people.

The New Testament is only slightly more forthcoming on Israel's history during its final days—the days following the Silent Years. The Jews are present in its pages, but the text contains too little information to facilitate reconstruction of ancient Israel's final chapter, for it focuses on Jesus' life and teachings and his followers' activities. To learn about ancient Israel's demise and gain insight into the first-century historical context of the Christian church's birth, one must look elsewhere. This work has addressed both themes by following the actions of the prefects and procurators who governed Judea from Herod's passing to Israel's dissolution in the First Roman War.

At Herod's death Judea was at the apex of its "grandeur and prosperity."[5] Relations between the Judeans and the Roman governors, except for Pontius Pilate's term (26–36), were fairly stable for several decades following

---

4. Matt 2:1–8, 13–16.
5. Goodman, *Rome and Jerusalem*, 33.

Archelaus's removal, in part because the province was still basking in the afterglow of Herodian prosperity. The governing prefects, if undistinguished for their administrative ability, were adequate for the task. Coponius (6–9) avoided renewed violence when Judas, the radical Galilean nationalist, advocated resisting Quirinius's census, for the clear-sighted high priest Joazar wisely convinced Judeans to comply, and the danger passed. The next three prefectorates encompassing the years 9 to 26 remained quiet and orderly.

There were recurring bouts of serious tension under Pontius Pilate, however, brought on largely by his low opinion of Jerusalem's religious community and his ill-considered actions. Bringing ensigns displaying the emperor's image and golden shields bearing inscriptions declaring his divinity into Jerusalem—something his predecessors avoided—ignored the Jews' monotheism and aversion to images. Violence and loss of life occurred after he dipped into temple funds without the council's approval. His removal, after violently repressing an imposter whom he suspected of harboring rebellious intentions in Samaria, briefly stabilized relations with Rome.

Interactions with the emperor reached a delicate impasse in the first century's fourth decade, when the unbalanced emperor Caligula infuriated Jerusalem by ordering his statue to be placed in the temple. The Syrian governor's judicious intervention, and Caligula's assassination, averted disaster. Conditions in Judea improved briefly under Agrippa I (41–44), but his promising reign was cut short by his untimely death. Judea reverted to being a Roman province governed by procurators stationed at Caesarea Maritima. Cuspius Fadus and Tiberius Alexander, the two procurators succeeding Agrippa, encountered minimal controversy with their subjects and their terms (44–48) were mainly peaceful.

Around midcentury, however, Judea entered a time of unrest that grew steadily worse over the next two decades. Appallingly unfit to govern, the procurators' mismanagement and moral vacuity permitted brigandage and disorder to grow virtually unchecked, eventually fanning the long-smoldering anti-Roman sentiment into the open flame of hopeless rebellion. Cummanus, procurator 48–52, repeatedly mishandled events during his term and was removed in disgrace. Felix (52–60) encountered nearly continuous trouble with agitators and charlatans and Jerusalem's civic disorder, while radical nationalists harassed the countryside and sicarii terrorized festivals. He escaped punishment for his harsh treatment of Caesarea Maritima Jews only by the emperor's brother's intervention. Conditions demanded strong and clear-sighted leadership when Albinus (62–64) became procurator, but his incompetence and exploitation of his position for personal gain accelerated Judea's deterioration. Fearful of being charged before the emperor on his return to Rome, he sought to endear himself to Judeans by executing all prisoners guilty of serious crimes, while permitting relatives of those held for lesser malfeasance to buy their freedom. The prisons were emptied, many criminals were released, while he profited handsomely.

With procurators guilty of administrative ineptitude and squalid morals governing Judea, the resistance to Rome, smoldering beneath the surface since the days of Archelaus and Judas the Galilean, intensified after midcentury. It took numerous forms: the rising number of radical nationalists—the Zealots—openly opposing Rome, increasingly violent outbreaks in the cities, recurring sicarii attacks, and the propensity of stressed and insecure Judeans to be enticed by the sham nostrums of charlatans and impostors.

These were combustible conditions requiring careful handling, but in the hands of Florus, Albinus's successor, forceful management and administrative integrity virtually disappeared. His legendary corruption surpassed even the turpitude of his predecessors. Robbery and disorder had free reign so long as it profited him. Tension flared in 66 when the Jews of Caesarea Maritima, learning that Nero would not intervene to protect their rights, withdrew from the city. Open rebellion erupted shortly in the tumult engulfing Jerusalem, after Florus removed funds from the temple treasury. When crowds openly taunted him, he turned soldiers loose to plunder a district of Jerusalem causing much loss of life. Enraged Jerusalemites occupied the temple and blocked access to the adjoining Antonia Fortress to prevent its soldiers from attacking. Without enough forces to control the situation, Florus withdrew to Caesarea, and Agrippa II's appeal to the rebels to abandon their cause failed, for they were no longer willing to accept Rome's authority. Ending the temple's daily sacrifices for the emperor marked the final break with Rome. Outright warfare soon followed, bringing Jerusalem's destruction and Israel's ultimate dissolution four years later.

This turbulent closing chapter of ancient Israel's history, extending from Herod's death to the destruction of Jerusalem, coincided with Christianity's birth. Judea's troubled political atmosphere—tension within Jerusalem's religious community, the increasingly volatile interaction with the province's Roman governors—constitute the background against which the events in the New Testament account occurred. The New Testament protagonists were bound to be affected by this context, but the impact of its political forces is easily overlooked, for they are only marginally evident in the biblical account. Jesus and his followers were not political activists looking to influence provincial affairs. Their concern was with matters leading to Christianity's birth, but, as they pursued their task, avoiding the political events roiling their surroundings was impossible.

Glimpses of how first-century Judea's political dynamics affected participants in the story of Christianity's birth are evident in the encounters of Paul, James the brother of Jesus, Stephen, and Jesus, with the province's authorities and religious leaders. Paul, after leaving the island of Rhodes, had gone to Jerusalem. While preparing to sacrifice in the temple an angry crowd of Asian Jews attacked him. They claimed he was arousing anti-Jewish sentiment and hostility to the law and the temple wherever he went, and mistakenly believed that he had defiled the temple by accompanying Greeks there. The crowd would have killed him if soldiers, probably from the adjacent Antonia Fortress, had not intervened. Uncertain why the Jews were hostile to Paul, himself a Jew, the Jerusalem tribune Lysias decided to question him and ordered a flogging beforehand, believing presumably that it would ensure that he would answer truthfully. As the flogging was about to begin, Paul startled the supervising centurion by questioning the legality of whipping an unconvicted Roman citizen. The alarmed officer immediately informed Lysias. When Paul confirmed his Roman citizenship, the tribune recognized his vulnerability; he had almost flogged a Roman citizen, information that could result in severe discipline if it reached the procurator Felix, the official to whom he was responsible.

Still wanting to learn what these Jews had against Paul, Lysias brought him before the Jerusalem council for questioning where, while defending himself, he revealed that he was a Pharisee. When the Pharisee scribes exonerated Paul, it divided the council's Pharisees and Sadducees so intensely that violence threatened, and fearing for Paul's safety the tribune lodged him in the barracks. Some prominent Jews, with the chief priests' and elders' complicity, then laid plans to kill Paul. Learning of their plot, Lysias opted to refer the matter to Felix and sent Paul to Caesarea Maritima at night under military escort.

At Paul's appearance before Felix, his accusers charged him with agitating his countrymen wherever he went, profaning the temple, and being a ringleader of the Nazarene sect. He denied exciting crowds in the temple and Jerusalem's synagogues, insisting that he was completing purification rites in preparation for sacrifice when the crowd accosted him. He affirmed his worship of the God of the Jews' ancestors and reverence for the law and the prophetic writings. Felix postponed settling the case until Lysias had testified, and kept Paul incarcerated with a modicum of freedom. He questioned Paul repeatedly but deferred his release, not questioning whether he had violated provincial law but because he expected to be paid to free him. That Paul's interrogation could incite a life-threatening clash between the Pharisees and Sadducees reveals how volatile the climate was even within the Jerusalem religious community, not to mention the tension in Judea's relationship with Rome. The episode shows Paul's dual vulnerability—to the Jerusalem religious community's political dynamics and to the imperial system that permitted an unscrupulous procurator to use his judicial authority for his personal benefit. He was still in custody two years later when Felix was recalled to Rome.[6]

The case of James, the brother of Jesus, is another example of early Judean Christians' vulnerability to the province's political system. When the procurator Festus died suddenly, the high priest Ananus brazenly exceeded his authority by trying James before the Sanhedrin for violating the law (as we saw in the preceding chapter). James was found guilty and stoned. This was a serious breach of high priestly authority, for the death penalty was the Judean procurator's prerogative. Had Festus not died, leaving the procuratorial office temporarily vacant, it is unlikely that James would have been executed, for in Roman officialdom's eyes violating the Jewish law did not warrant levying the death sentence. James was the victim of a dictatorial high priest who, when the opportunity presented itself during a procuratorial vacancy, presumptuously assumed the Roman governor's authority.

Stephen suffered a similar fate. He was responsible for distributing aid to needy gentile widows among Jerusalem's Christian community, and encountered serious opposition from the city's Synagogue of the Freedmen. When he was brought before the council, suborned witnesses accused him of blasphemy. During his defense he charged the religious leaders with killing the "Righteous One," Jesus, just as their ancestors had murdered the prophets. An enraged crowd seized him, and without a formal trial or referring the matter to the governor, stoned him. As in the case of James, there is no evidence of the governor taking any punitive action following Stephen's death, although it was a clear violation of his death sentence prerogative.

Jesus' treatment by the Judean political order provides additional insight into the context in which first-century Christians functioned. As

---

6. For the sequence of events leading to Paul's incarceration in Caesarea Maritima, see Acts 21:1–24, 27.

long as Jesus confined his ministry to Galilee, he encountered little trouble. When he came to Jerusalem, where there was ongoing conflict between Pontius Pilate and the religious community, it was another matter.

Jesus arrived in Jerusalem during Passover, when the city was crowded with visitors. The feast offered hostile elements a prime opportunity to arouse the anti-Roman sentiment never far below the surface of Judean life. Passover was always a tense time for the Roman authorities. Aware of the potential for disruptive incidents on these occasions, prefects, normally residing in Caesarea Maritima, moved to Herod's palace in Jerusalem, bringing extra soldiers to be on hand should trouble occur. When a large crowd welcomed Jesus with a triumphal procession, it alarmed the Jerusalem religious elite. His ability to attract sizable numbers revealed his popularity and aroused their jealousy and fear. Jesus was known to be from Galilee, the home of Judas, the anti-tax rebel active during the Quirinius census, and Galilee itself had a reputation for being unruly. The religious leaders undoubtedly suspected that Jesus was another troublesome northern agitator whose popularity signaled that an uprising could be afoot. Rumors circulated that Jesus opposed paying taxes to Rome—a serious offense—and giving substance to those stories was the fact that he had convinced Matthew, a Capernaum tax collector, to leave his position. Jesus also had been entertained by Zacchaeus, Jericho's chief tax collector. Other reports alleged that he claimed to be king of the Jews. In Judea, where resistance to Rome was easily awakened, opposing Roman taxes and harboring political aspirations made one dangerous and an easy target. To the Jerusalem religious elite, Jesus was dangerous on two counts. His popularity threatened their entrenched position. The religious leaders, who had already witnessed Pilate's use of force against Judeans, also feared that Jesus might give him reason to resort to harsh measures again. Charging Jesus before Pilate for arousing Jews with his political ambitions and opposition to taxes would remove both dangers. Complying with the Jerusalem leaders' request to kill Jesus also conveniently served Pilate's interest; by accommodating their demands, he undoubtedly hoped to ease tension and repair relations with his restless Judean subjects. In these circumstances, Jesus was a pawn sacrificed to the political order's needs.

This overview of the political forces shaping first-century Judea sheds light on one aspect of the New Testament context. Exploring Judea's socioeconomic dynamics would further illuminate the background against which the New Testament unfolds, but regrettably that is beyond the scope of this work.

XI

Reflection

HAVING CROSSED THE FOUR-HUNDRED-YEAR bridge spanning the biblical canon's gap between the Old and New Testaments, it remains to consider what relevance, if any, Israel's experience in the Silent Years has for twenty-first-century Christians.

About a century after Israel's return from Babylon, as we have seen, Alexander established an empire extending eastward from Greece to India's borders that facilitated Greek culture's spread to Judea. This cultural intrusion affected Judeans. They interacted with civil officers and traders in their province from hellenized neighboring kingdoms. Hellenistic mores became increasingly evident. Judeans began using Greek names, celebrating Greek holidays, minting coins with Greek inscriptions, and using funerary monuments with Greek forms.

In the hellenized cities surrounding Jerusalem public buildings displayed classic elements of Greek culture, pillars, colonnades, and porticoes. With no distinctive architectural style of their own, Judeans borrowed these features to dress prominent buildings—the Antonia palace-fortress, the Hasmonean palace, and Herod's palace. Even the temple complex incorporated Hellenistic traits; its overall plan relied on a Greek model, while porticoes lined three of its inner walls, and a stoa lay along the fourth. Its main function was accommodating religious ritual, but, following Greek custom, the temple also served as an agora or marketplace, facilitating numerous social and economic activities.

The hellenized cities also provided a variety of entertainment for their residents. Artistic performances filled their theaters and amphitheaters, and gymnasiums, stadiums, and hippodromes were venues for camaraderie, exercise, and watching bloody spectacles, or youths train for the games. These characteristic features of Greek life would not have escaped the attention of Judeans. Jerusalem itself acquired a gymnasium even before the Hasmonean uprising, and Herod eventually added a theater and amphitheater, possibly a hippodrome, and instituted the city's Actian Games.

Greek became the region's *lingua franca*, opening the door to careers in commerce, government, and the army, and to Greek science, philosophy, history, drama, and mythology, for upper-class youths. The Greek mind questioned superstition and religious explanation, and relied on reason and observation to answer life's great questions and decode the material world. For young Judeans nurtured by the synagogue's instruction in the Torah and the temple's ritual—traditions anchored in revelation that accounted for the universe and gave life meaning—Greek learning undoubtedly was heady fare, not to mention the attraction of the gymnasium, stadium, and games.

By the mid-second century Greek culture clearly had made significant inroads into Judean life. Hebrew writers, as we have seen, lamented its destructive impact. Much to the satisfaction of the extreme hellenizers, the high priest Menelaus even cooperated with Antiochus Epiphanes in implementing the "Abomination of Desolation." This precipitated the Hasmonean rebellion, forcing the offensive decrees to be withdrawn. Their repeal undoubtedly was an immediate setback for the hellenizers, but in the long run did little to impede Judea's hellenization.

Energized by nationalism, and the desire to restore Israel's religious traditions, the Hasmonean rebels pressed their cause and by 142 achieved *de facto* independence. Two years later Judeans installed Simon as high priest and military head in a public event of great significance, for it marked the restoration of Israel's independence after four centuries of domination by foreign powers. His investiture took place in Jerusalem, witnessed by Jewish leaders and the assembled people.

Surprisingly, however, Hebrew custom was ignored in the ceremony, for, had it been followed, in all likelihood the assembly would have marked Simon's installation by swearing an oath of allegiance to him. Instead, a uniquely Greek document implemented his investiture. It opened with a statement explaining the reasons for the step about to be taken, to which a proclamation conveying authority to Simon was attached. Elias Bickerman,

Reflection

a twentieth-century historian of the Second Temple era, writes that the document was "thoroughly Hellenistic" in form and likely written in Greek and further insists that it could not have occurred in Hebrew tradition.[1] Inaugurating the renewal of Israel's independence using Greek rather than customary Hebrew forms was a remarkable departure in protocol, poignantly indicating the extent to which Judeans had absorbed Greek culture.

The Greek manner of Simon's investiture was a harbinger of the Hasmonean conduct that would follow in later decades. The Jerusalem cultus (high priest, temple, and sacrificial ritual) survived, but increasingly Israel's court modeled itself on its hellenized neighbors. Hyrcanus I (134–04) concentrated on extending his kingdom. Relying on mercenaries because of his unpopularity, he seized territory across the Jordan and in Samaria before annexing Idumea and grafting its population into Judaism through compulsory circumcision. He intended his wife to succeed him, but his son Aristobulus (104–03) seized the throne. He imprisoned three of his brothers and his mother—he arranged her death by starvation—before suspicion led him to kill a fourth brother. The degenerate Alexander Jannaeus (103–76) murdered a brother to gain the throne, and, after losing his subjects' support, relied on brutal force to sustain his position, and was constantly at war. His hellenized court's ostentatious secular opulence antagonized the Hasidim, and by assuming the title of king he threatened the Sanhedrin's customary authority. When rebellion erupted he crucified eight hundred dissidents and slew their wives and children before them as they died while he caroused with courtesans. Exhausted by dissolute living, he died prematurely. His sons, Aristobulus II (67–63) and Hyrcanus II (63–40), then fought each other for the throne.

These later Hasmoneans bore little resemblance to their spirited predecessors, who overthrew the Seleucids to restore Israel's nationhood and religious traditions. They disregarded their ancestors' solemn vows made in the days of Ezra and Nehemiah, to "walk in God's law . . . and observe all the commandments of the Lord,"[2] to say nothing of the model of behavior Moses prescribed for Israel's kings in Deuteronomy:

> When he has taken the throne of his kingdom, he [the king] shall have a copy of this law written for him in the presence of the Levitical priests. It shall remain with him and he shall read in it all the days of his life, so that he may learn to fear the Lord his God,

---

1. Bickerman, *From Ezra to the Last of the Maccabees*, 157.
2. Neh 10:29.

diligently observing all the words of this law and these statutes, neither exalting himself above other members of the community nor turning aside from the commandment, either to the right or the left, so that he and his descendants may reign long over his kingdom in Israel.[3]

A "new, foreign, and technologically superior" civilization's attraction proved irresistible to Second Temple Jews, Bickerman concludes, and "acted . . . as a powerful dissolvent which destroyed the traditional discipline of [Hebrew] life."[4] The Hasmoneans succumbed to the insidious influence of Greek civilization that had impinged on Judean life since the days of Alexander. They became virtually indistinguishable from their hellenized neighbors. Accommodation with Hellenism wasn't the only factor in their deflection from Israel's tradition, but it was a major contributor to the later Hasmoneans' recreancy.

Twenty-first century people leave esoteric topics like hippodromes and amphitheaters, hellenized kingdoms and decadent Hasmoneans, high priests and the temple, incompetent and corrupt Roman prefects and procurators, to scholars and eccentric antiquarians. Smartphones and iPads, databanks and privacy, hackers and terrorists, robots and artificial intelligence, mortgages, student loans, and climate change hold their attention. Discerning believers, however, might profit from knowing of the Second Temple Jews' interface with Greek culture. Like ancient Judeans, they live in a society infused with postmodernism, a cultural influence dismissive of cardinal principles of their faith. Postmodernism emerged during the twentieth century's later decades. Perceiving the nature of its challenge for believers, however, requires insight into the meaning of modernism, for postmodernism is an outlook that grew as a reaction to modernism, a worldview that emerged in the wake of the Enlightenment.

Modernism grew from the coalescence of ideas gestating for centuries in Western civilization.[5] The medieval world, relying on revelation and the scholasticism of Thomas Aquinas, sought to distill understanding of its world from the biblical canon. Renaissance thinkers saw the Greek and Roman past as a great repository of wisdom and knowledge; venerating the humanist values celebrated in classical antiquity's literature, they held

---

3. Deut 17:18–20.
4. Bickerman, *From Ezra to the Last of the Maccabees*, 59.
5. Grenz, *Primer on Postmodernism*, 57–81.

Reflection

an elevated view of humanity's place in the universe.[6] The Renaissance also fostered interest in the natural order. Francis Bacon, the late Renaissance philosopher and scientist, however, unlike his Renaissance predecessors, questioned the veracity of knowledge handed down from ancient sources. As an empiricist, he sought to understand the material world through observation and experimentation. The scientific method of investigation, he believed, could decode the universe and reveal nature's secrets.[7]

The Enlightenment, following pathways indicated by the Baconian process, gave priority to humanity's rational endowment in pursuing knowledge of the existing world.[8] Like Bacon, the seventeenth-century philosopher and mathematician Rene Descartes refused to rely on knowledge handed down from antiquity, but neither was he content with the quality of information the scientific method offered. Desiring to devise a way of knowing which yielded knowledge that was indisputably true, he turned to mathematics. Mathematical truths, he believed, were more certain than the conclusions generated by the empirical methods of science, for they could be faulty since they depended on sensory perception. He began by doubting everything except that which he knew with certainty to be true, and came to the conclusion that there was only one thing that a thinking person could not doubt: one's existence. It was encapsulated in his famous dictum: "I think, therefore I am."

Descartes's work set the stage for the Enlightenment. Released from the inadequacy of relying on knowledge inherited from the classical past and the scientific method's alleged shortcomings, the Enlightenment freed the individual to rely on humanity's rational dimension in the process of knowing. The Enlightenment—the Age of Reason—made reason the main arbiter in the pursuit of truth.[9]

Subsequently, physicist and mathematician Isaac Newton (lived 1642–1727) redirected the investigative/knowing process back to the scientific method. His observations and calculations led him to discover gravity and the laws of motion. He likened the universe to a great machine, functioning according to laws. These could be known, he believed, by applying the scientific method. They would provide knowledge, enabling humans to

---

6. Grenz, *Primer on Postmodernism*, 58, 60.
7. Grenz, *Primer on Postmodernism*, 58–59.
8. Grenz, *Primer on Postmodernism*, 62.
9. Grenz, *Primer on Postmodernism*, 63–65, 80–81.

understand the forces of nature and use them to improve their quality of life.[10] The perceptiveness of Newton's farsighted prediction was apparent by the late nineteenth century. Science, with its successes in unveiling the material order's secrets, together with technology, its offspring, was providing a rich trove of devices capable of doing useful work that eased life for humans.

The achievements of science in revealing nature's secrets inspired behaviorists to apply science's quantitative methods to the study of society and human behavior.[11] This raised the possibility that human behavior, like the natural order, was subject to universal laws. Social reformers and social workers entertained hope that this would unveil society's dynamics and lead to useful ways of improving the social conditions under which humans live.

Belief in humanity's elevated position in the universe, confidence in the autonomous individual's rationality, certainty that science and technology would continue enhancing the conditions of human life, and anticipation that behaviorists were about to find the key to improving the social order's functioning—these beliefs had gained widespread credence throughout the Western world by the late nineteenth century.

The modernist worldview assumes that an objective, unified external world exists which functions according to natural laws. It claims this knowledge can be accessed by impartial, rational searchers, using reason and the tools of science. This pursuit is desirable, modernists believed, for it benefits humankind. They further imagined Western civilization to be on the cusp of a fecund new era in which enlightened humans would order their lives with rationality; the empirical methods of science would be the accepted means of acquiring knowledge and accessing reality. Whatever could not withstand quantitative testing could be safely discarded. (This was a core tenet of modernism, and, in some circles, virtually a transcendent truth.[12]) Science and technology's ongoing interaction would continue easing life's rigors, and the social order, resonating with the behaviorists' anticipated discoveries, would experience great improvement. Continuous progress would characterize the new day. Theologian Stanley Grenz succinctly summarized the essence of modernism's roots and thrust. "From Francis Bacon to the present," he wrote,

---

10. Grenz, *Primer on Postmodernism*, 67, 80–81.
11. Grenz, *Primer on Postmodernism*, 59.
12. Grenz, *Primer on Postmodernism*, 50.

Reflection

> The goal of the human intellectual quest has been to unlock the secrets of the universe in order to master nature for human benefit and create a better world. This Enlightenment quest, in turn, produced the modern technological society of the twentieth century. At the heart of this society is the desire to rationally manage life, on the assumption that scientific advancement and technology provide the means to improving the quality of human life.[13]

The following century, however, proved to be stony ground for the seeds of hope modernists planted so optimistically. Rather than yielding a bountiful harvest of human progress, their seedlings were stunted by the carnage of World War I's trenches, machine guns, poison gas, and submarines. Some went to war believing it to be a conflict that would finally end war and make the world safe for democracy permanently by establishing an international parliament—the League of Nations; it would obviate war by implementing the rule of law among nations. The League, however, failed to halt the armed conflicts of the 1930s. World War II followed with the aerial destruction of cities and their populations, loss of some fifty million lives, the barbarities of the Holocaust, and ended with a demonstration of nuclear warfare's catastrophic potential. Then the Cold War saw nuclear-armed powers locked in threatening postures, their apocalyptic destructive capability held in check by the fear of mutually assured annihilation should either attack. The twentieth century undeniably witnessed significant advances—in medical skills, the ease and speed of travel, space exploration, and the gathering, transmission, and analysis of data, for example. These developments, however, fell far short of modernism's roseate expectations, for a vast expansion of human destructive capability accompanied them, to say nothing of the self-imposed scourge of drug dependency that enveloped the Western world.

By midcentury these developments were casting an ominous shadow over modernism's vision. Moreover, substantive grounds for questioning modernism's hope existed in the work of the late-nineteenth-century philosopher Friedrich Nietzsche. Nietzsche denied that reason and philosophical inquiry—the twin pillars supporting the Enlightenment project—offered humans access to reality. He understood the world to consist of a vast number of bits, each different from all others. In their search to know reality, humans arrange them in categories. Nietzsche believed this to be a fundamental error, for it ignores each fragment's unique features, obscuring

---

13. Grenz, *Primer on Postmodernism*, 81.

its true reality. He used the relationship of the general category of "leaf" to individual leaves as an example to clarify his meaning. Individual leaves share many traits, yet each leaf is unique. To speak of leaves in general, he declared, hides each leaf's singularity, resulting in a false perception of its true nature.[14] Creating categories of knowledge in the Enlightenment manner in order to know reality, Nietzsche concluded, inevitably distorts reality. What passes for human knowledge, he claimed, is merely a set of illusions that humans themselves construct.[15] Essentially, Nietzsche held that humans cannot access reality or perceive the "true world."[16] In Nietzsche's view, the grand Enlightenment quest—finding reality by applying reason and philosophical inquiry to the knowing process, the foundation on which modernism's expectations rested—was a pointless quest.

As midcentury confidence in modernism's auspicious vision waned, a reaction set in. It induced the rise of "postmodernism," an outlook that challenges the foundation on which modernism rests and permeates the world of twenty-first-century believers.

A trio of French philosophers spearheaded postmodernism's emergence. Michele Foucault shared Nietzsche's skepticism of the Enlightenment project. The Enlightenment's means of accessing reality, in his judgment, was irremediably flawed. As we have seen, it assumes the existence of an objective body of knowledge about a unified external world, waiting for impartial searchers to access, using reason and the scientific method. Their findings supposedly open the door to knowledge of the world and are true representations of material reality. Modernist heirs of the Enlightenment mantle believe they possess such information, that it is objectively true, and its pursuit is a worthy endeavor benefiting humankind and ensuring progress.

Foucault rejected these claims. In his opinion, an impartial observer/knower is an illusion, for humans have no access to a point beyond society and history from which to make objective observations.[17] All perceptions, therefore, he concluded, are embedded in society and history, and reflect interests existing where they occur. Claiming truth to be objective and verifiable by appropriate scholarly research is invalid; in fact, he declared truth to be a product of the power system that makes it possible and nothing more

---

14. Grenz, *Primer on Postmodernism*, 89.
15. Grenz, *Primer on Postmodernism*, 90.
16. Grenz, *Primer on Postmodernism*, 91.
17. Grenz, *Primer on Postmodernism*, 131.

than fiction.[18] Impartial science was impossible for, in his view, science was "ideology." Neither could history legitimately claim to be energized by a neutral wish for knowledge of the past, for he believed it was rooted in a desire to justify the existing power structure. As for the social sciences, they offered no evidence for the existence of an entity that could be called "human nature" ruled by "lawlike regularities," as behaviorists imagined. Essentially Foucault, and the postmodernism his work fostered, was devoid of confidence in human knowledge.[19]

Jacques Derrida, Foucault's compatriot, repudiated the Enlightenment's means of accessing reality by discrediting the "realist" school of language on which modernism depended. The "realists" hold that humans possess the capacity to acquire understanding of the world as it actually exists and assume the language they use to describe it has a direct, one-to-one relation with objects in the real world and the entire natural order.[20] Derrida and the postmodernists, however, are devotees of the "constructionist" school of language. It sees language as a convention formed in a constantly changing social context; humans use it to "construct" meaning rather than reveal an objective meaning already existing in the world. In effect, Derrida claims that the external world humans describe is an artificial structure they create. Their descriptive statements, therefore, are not true representations of the external world, as the realist school and the modernists hold, for language has no direct connection with a fixed external reality. Furthermore, he seems to say that a text's meaning is not found in what the author deposits in it; rather, meaning occurs when a reader engages with it. In other words, a text's meaning is determined by what the reader brings to it; it can vary with each reading and every new reader who confronts it. In Derrida's view, even if a fixed external reality was accessible (which Nietzsche and Foucault deny), language lacks the ability to describe it or convey a constant truth about it.[21]

Postmodernists also invoked anthropological knowledge to discredit modernism. Twentieth-century anthropological insight claims that myths are more than tales that primitive folk celebrate. They are expressions of a society's core values, the beliefs anchoring its social relationships. They

---

18. Grenz, *Primer on Postmodernism*, 133.
19. Grenz, *Primer on Postmodernism*, 123.
20. Grenz, *Primer on Postmodernism*, 40–41.
21. Grenz, *Primer on Postmodernism*, 139–42.

are the incorporeal ligaments holding societies together by affirming and validating their existence. Postmodernists call them "metanarratives."[22]

So, postmodernists would say, in the post-Enlightenment world modernists imagined they were building a new order forged in rationality that would free the contemporary world from the myths and superstitions they believed responsible for the conflicts and wars of premodern times. This would improve the human condition and ensure advancement. The new order modernists envisioned was rooted in a "metanarrative of progress."

As postmodernist thought was emerging and as some twentieth-century historical realities unfolded, however, confidence in the Modernist vision withered, as we have noted. Jean Francois Lyotard, the postmodernist trio's third member, asserted there was more sapping the modernist vision than the century's troubling events. He believed history naturally passes through stages when one controlling myth displaces another. Post-midcentury society, he claimed, had entered a phase in which belief in all metanarratives had collapsed, for, in his opinion, the concept of the great metanarrative was no longer credible to the late-twentieth-century mind.[23] The force that had propelled the Enlightenment and inspired the modernist vision had lost its appeal.

Postmodernism and the Christian faith obviously have sharply contrasting outlooks. As Stanley Grenz has made clear, postmodernists have no confidence in human knowledge, for humans cannot perceive reality in their world.[24] The Christian perspective is different. Christians believe that a rational God created humans in his image (Gen 1:2, 9:6). Bearing his image, they have been endowed with ability to reason. Their reasoning power is far below God's rationality and was damaged in the fall, but it was not obliterated. Even in its flawed condition it enables humans to perceive reality. Employing reason and the scientific method—tools available to human rationality—they can pursue knowledge of the setting in which God placed them. That knowledge is not flawless or complete, but neither is it fiction, as postmodernists assert. Its all-too-frequent misuse notwithstanding, it has contributed much to humanity's comfort and constantly undergoes testing, refinement, and growth. Moreover, despite its limitations, it has been able to reveal profound insights into the infinite dimensions of God's unparalleled greatness.

22. Grenz, *Primer on Postmodernism*, 44.
23. Grenz, *Primer on Postmodernism*, 44–46.
24. Grenz, *Primer on Postmodernism*, 123.

Reflection

Postmodernists, conceding that truth, like human knowledge, is a casualty of humanity's inability to access reality, and asserting that no location is free of influence from the competing forces within society, claim objective perceptions of the surrounding world are impossible. What appears to be truth might be the end product of competition among society's contending forces and arguably indistinguishable from fiction. Even if truth did exist and could be accessed by humans, however, postmodernists insist language could not accommodate it. In their world spoken language is a convention or custom that humans use to "construct" meaning rather than convey truth about existing objects. It has limited connection with the external order. And postmodernists claim written words are equally unable to convey truth. Their function is limited to connecting the reader's mind with text, not transmitting what the author lodged in it. Does not postmodernism also warn that what passes for truth may be little more than the fruit of artful imagination?

The claim that truth is impossible because humans can't perceive reality does not comport with believers' outlook. Their God is the eternal creator who existed before creation and the inauguration of time. While having access to time, he exists beyond time and its limitations, and his observations are impervious to the social forces postmodernists claim deny humans access to reality and decimate truth. God's observation point is objective. His observations are authoritative and reliable, and he has communicated them to humans through Scripture, for unlike postmodernists, God has full confidence in language. God speaks. He summoned creation into existence (Gen 1:1–3). He called Abraham and covenanted with him (Gen 12:1–3, 7). After summoning Moses and commissioning him to lead the Israelites from Egypt and covenanting with them in the wilderness, he directed the implementation of the law, as the book of Exodus records in detail. God also writes. He inscribed a code of conduct on stone for the Israelites as they were about to enter Canaan and become a nation (Exod 20:1–17, 31:18, 34:1). Through the agency of the Holy Spirit, he entrusted a revelation of himself to a book of instruction for human guidance (the Holy Bible). He even embedded his word in flesh, that it might fulfill its mission as the eternal light that shines in the darkness, to redeem penitent humans and establish his kingdom (John 1:1–5).

A great divide also exists between the outlooks of the postmodernists and Christian believers over the role of metanarrative. Postmodernists insist that the metanarrative idea is outdated and has lost its credibility for contemporary society. The believer's faith, however, is inextricably linked to a grand story. It begins with the eternal God summoning into existence his good creation. Although his creatures disfigure it with their disobedience, the loving God calls Abraham and covenants with him, promising that in his descendants all humans will be blessed. The narrative of his ongoing relations with his chosen people reveals much about God's nature and what he requires of his creatures. The Messiah's advent—God's word made flesh—sacrificial death and resurrection, provides for God's penitent creatures to be reconciled to right relation with himself and ultimately the establishment of the kingdom God planned from the beginning where he will dwell with his people. It is a grand story, a glorious metanarrative of hope and faith.

The postmodern outlook has implications for Christian believers. If, as postmodernism insists, language cannot convey knowledge veraciously, and humanity has no access to valid knowledge of the world it inhabits, truth, an essential ingredient of the believers' outlook, is not a realistic objective. It seems this claim is gaining acceptance in some quarters. Witness the disposition to grant recognition, even legitimacy, to the multiplicity of delusionary rumors circulating on social media or the enduring fascination with unsubstantiated conspiracy theories. Among those prepared to allot truth a diminished role, this reflects an affinity for the postmodern proposition that truth and fiction are indistinguishable. Over time this has the potential to undermine the outlook of believers, already a minority in the larger society.

Young believers are not impervious to the issues the postmodern outlook raises. As today's students, they constantly hear the "truth is relative" (to time and place) refrain among their fellow learners, as Allan Bloom notes.[25] As leaders of tomorrow's believers, will they still celebrate the metanarrative of hope and faith their parents cherished, or see it as a quaint relic of the premodern myths and superstitions that modernists hoped to replace with their metanarrative of progress? The later Hasmoneans, as we have seen, gradually lost sight of the grand story as they encountered Greek culture. Second Temple Jews succeeded in preserving the Jerusalem cultus (high priest, temple, and sacrificial ritual), but their court adopted the corrupt ways of neighboring hellenized kingdoms. They strayed far from the

---

25. The American philosopher Allan Bloom, as cited by Greer, *Mapping Postmodernism*, 13, in his book *The Closing of the American Mind*, writes, "There is one thing a professor can be absolutely certain of: almost every student entering the university believes, or says he believes, that truth is relative."

Reflection

model of royal behavior Moses prescribed, and post-exile Israel covenanted to uphold in the days of Ezra and Nehemiah. As twenty-first-century Christians encounter postmodernism, consideration of Israel's experience with Greek culture may be instructive.

Questions for Focus and Discussion

CHAPTER ONE

1. Where were the centers of power in the Jews' world as they began returning from the Babylonian exile?

2. What position do these two ancient powers occupy in today's world, and how do they relate to Israel?

3. When did the Jews begin returning to Judea from Babylon, and how long did this migration continue?

4. Which figures led the returns, and which one made the greatest contribution to the process?

5. What is your assessment of the treatment of the "foreign" women with children whom earlier returnees had married?

Questions for Focus and Discussion

6. Christians believe the Jews were God's chosen channel for revealing himself to humanity. Can you suggest a reason for the four-hundred-year gap in their biblical story extending from their return from Babylonian captivity to their reappearance in the New Testament?

7. Should Christians bother with learning about the Jews' history during this gap?

CHAPTER TWO

1. Why could Macedon defeat Greece when Persia failed?

2. Who was Alexander the Great, and why is he called "the Great?"

3. When did Alexander's empire exist, and what accounts for his remarkable success in building it in a mere dozen years?

4. What became of Alexander's empire after his death, and how was Israel impacted?

CHAPTER THREE

1. What was the permanent legacy of Alexander's short-lived empire?

2. What does the term "Hellenism" mean?

Questions for Focus and Discussion

3. Can you describe some of the main features of classical Greek civilization?

4. In what key way were classical Greeks unique among the peoples of their era?

5. Identify Plato, Aristotle, Zeno, and Epicurus, and briefly describe one or two main features of their outlooks.

6. How did Second Temple Jews respond to Hellenism?

7. Some commentators have said classical Greeks would feel at home in contemporary North America. Do you agree?

CHAPTER FOUR

1. What are the approximate dates of the Maccabean (Hasmonean) interlude in Israel's history?

2. Identify the "abomination of desolation." Why would it be such a great offense to Jewish people?

3. Identify Judas Maccabaeus, and describe his role in the Maccabean rebellion.

Questions for Focus and Discussion

4. Who was Jonathan Maccabaeus? What was his contribution to the Maccabean rebellion?

5. Who was Simon Maccabaeus? Explain his role in the Maccabean interlude.

6. Do you see any similarities between Israel's position in the Silent Years and Israel's position in the contemporary world?

CHAPTER FIVE

1. In a sentence or two, characterize the governance of each of the four later Hasmonean rulers: Hyrcanus I, Aristobulus, Jannai, and Alexandra Salome.

2. Comment on the outcome when Queen Alexandra Salome died without leaving a designated successor.

CHAPTER SIX

1. Who was Pompey? How did his actions affect Second Temple Jews?

2. Was the Maccabean interlude in Second Temple Jewish history a success or a failure, or would you characterize it in some other way?

Questions for Focus and Discussion

3. Do you think Antipater's brief appearance in Second Temple history merits consideration?

CHAPTER SEVEN

1. Comment on the challenges Herod encountered in establishing his authority at the outset of his Judean reign.

2. Mark Antony and Octavian (Augustus) were figures requiring Herod's careful attention. Why?

3. Account for the introduction of the Actian Games. Why were they controversial?

4. Which one among the many projects in Herod's extensive building program was the most memorable? Explain your choice. Can you identify some of the distinguishing characteristics of Herod's building program?

5. Do you see any significant differences between the early and late stages of Herod's reign?

6. In your view, was Herod a success or a failure as a king, or would you evaluate him in a different way?

Questions for Focus and Discussion

7. All things considered, in your view, what is most memorable about Herod?

8. Has your view of Herod changed?

CHAPTER EIGHT

1. What became of Herod's kingdom when he died?

CHAPTER NINE

1. What became of Judea following Archelaus's removal? How was it governed?

2. Among the various prefects and procurators who governed first-century-CE Palestine, which three would you say were most significant?

3. Could knowing about the history of the prefects and procurators who governed first-century Palestine have any value for Christians?

CHAPTER TEN

1. Can you locate the approximate time period of the Silent Years in the broad story of ancient Israel's history?

Questions for Focus and Discussion

2. If you were asked to make a general outline of Israel's history during the Silent Years, how might you divide the story into meaningful periods or stages?

3. Do you think Herod's death was a significant turning point in Israel's history?

4. In your view, how do conditions in first-century Judea before and after the century's mid-point compare?

5. Do you see any similarities between conditions in late-first-century Judea and conditions in twenty-first-century North America?

6. How did the political atmosphere in first-century Judea affect Christian leaders of the day?

CHAPTER ELEVEN

1. How did Hellenism influence Judean life during the Silent Years?

2. What do you see as the main features of the modernist outlook?

3. Why did the modernist vision experience considerable stress by the mid-twentieth century?

Questions for Focus and Discussion

4. Do you think the modernist outlook is defunct?

5. Can you explain briefly what any two of the following figures contributed to the birth of postmodernism: Friedrich Nietzsche, Michele Foucault, Jacques Derrida, and Francois Lyotard?

6. Where do postmodernism and Christianity clash?

7. Chapter 11 implies that Hellenism was to Second Temple Jews what postmodernism is to twenty-first-century Christians. Do you agree?

ANCIENT ISRAEL TIMELINE	
17th century BCE	Abraham leaves Ur. Settles in Canaan. Famine forces Israelites to Egypt where descendants are enslaved.
13th century	Moses leads exodus from Egypt. Ten Commandments received at Sinai.
ca. 1200–1100	Twelve tribes occupy Canaan. Judges rule.
ca. 1000	David forms united kingdom. Jerusalem capital. Solomon builds temple.
930	Kingdom divides into Judah and Israel when ten northern tribes secede.
722	Assyrians decimate Israel. Ten tribes exiled and lost.
586	Babylonians defeat Judah. Upper-class Judeans exiled to Babylon. Temple destroyed.
538	Persia defeats Babylon. Judea attached to Persia's "Province Beyond the River." Judean exiles begin homeward migration.
515	Temple rebuilt.
SILENT YEARS	
332–320	Alexander the Great conquers region.
ca. 300–200	Judea a vassal of Ptolemaic Egypt.
ca. 200–166	Judea a vassal of Seleucid Syria.
166–160	Maccabean rebellion.
142–129	Judean autonomy under Hasmoneans.
129–63	Judean independence under Hasmoneans.
63	Pompey captures Jerusalem. Judea becomes vassal of Roman Empire.
37–04 BCE	Judea a client kingdom of Rome, ruled by Herod.
6–66 CE	Herod's former kingdom becomes a minor Roman province governed by prefects and procurators.
66–70	Judea rebels. Defeated in First Roman War. Temple destroyed. High priestly office ends.

HASMONEAN DYNASTY	
Mattathias 167–166 BCE	Resisted Antiochus IV's religious decrees, sparking Maccabean rebellion. Gave rebellion's leadership to his son Judas before dying.
Judas (Maccabeas) 165–160	Led rebellion with guerrilla tactics. Concluded mutual assistance pact with Rome. Killed in battle with Syrians. Cleansed desecrated temple.
Jonathan 160–142	Judas's brother and successor. Restrained rebels by retreating to Tekoa to preserve their strength. Exploited Syrian disunity to promote Judean autonomy. Treacherously captured by Syrians and executed ca. 142.
Simon 142–134	Succeeded Jonathan, his brother, with popular approval. Secured Judean autonomy from Syria 142. Invested as high priest and military head by Judeans 140. Assassinated 134.
Hyrcanus (Johanan) 134–104	Simon's son. High priest and commander. Annexed Idumea. Captured territory east of Jordan River. Sympathetic to Sadducees.
Aristobulus 104–103	Hyrcanus's son. Seized power on Hyrcanus's death. Annexed Iturea. Died suddenly.
Jannaeus 103–76	Aristobulus's son. Priest and king. Hellenized court. Luxurious secular lifestyle. Constant war. Expansionist foreign policy. Crushed opposition ruthlessly. Died prematurely from dissolute living.
Alexandra Salome 76–67	Jannaeus's wife. Seized throne on Jannaeus's death. Preserved Hasmonean rule by expanding army but avoiding war. Cooperated with Pharisees. Died leaving no designated successor.
Hyrcanus II 67–63	Jannaeus's son. Hyrcanus II and Aristobulus II (brothers) battle for throne. With help of Antipater and Nabatean king, Hyrcanus II gains throne.

Herod the Great's Family

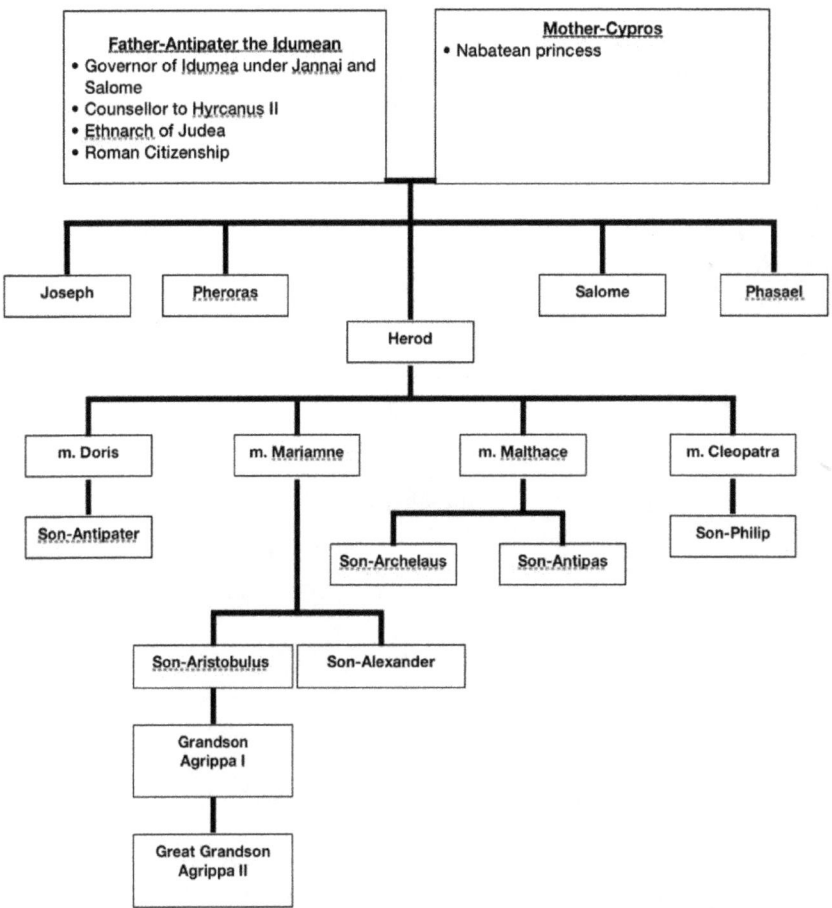

Bibliography

Actemeier, Paul J., et al. *Introducing the New Testament: Its Literature and Theology*. Grand Rapids: Eerdmans, 2001.
Bickerman, Elias. *From Ezra to the Last of the Maccabees: Foundations of Post-Biblical Judaism*. New York: Schoken, 1962.
———. *The Jews in the Greek Age*. Cambridge, MA: Harvard University Press, 1988.
Butler, Christopher. *Post-Modernism: A Very Short Introduction*. New York: Oxford University Press, 2002.
Cartledge, Paul. *Alexander the Great: The Hunt for a New Past*. New York: Overlook, 2004.
Durant, Will. *Caesar and Christ*. New York: Simon and Schuster, 1944.
———. *The Life of Greece*. New York: Simon and Schuster, 1939.
Ferguson, Everett. *Backgrounds of Early Christianity*. Grand Rapids: Eerdmans, 2003.
Gabba, Amilio. "The Finances of King Herod." In *Greece and Rome in Eretz Israel: Collected Essays*, edited by A. Kusher et al., 160-68. Jerusalem: Israel Exploration Society, 1990.
Gay, Peter. *Modernism: The Lure of Heresy, From Baudelaire to Becket and Beyond*. New York: W. W. Norton, 2008.
Goodman, Martin. *Rome and Jerusalem: The Clash of Ancient Civilizations*. London: Allen Lane, 2007.
Grant, Michael. *Herod the Great*. New York: American Heritage, 1971.
———. *The History of Ancient Israel*. New York: Charles Scribner's Sons, 1984.
Greer, Robert C. *Mapping Postmodernism: Survey of Christian Options*. Downers Grove: Intervarsity, 2003.
Grenz, Stanley J. *A Primer on Postmodernism*. Grand Rapids: Eerdmans, 1996.
Josephus, Flavius. *The Works of Josephus: New Updated Edition*. Translated by William Whiston. Peabody: Hendrickson, 1987.
LaSor, William Sanford, et al. *Old Testament Survey: The Message, Form and Background*. 2nd ed. Grand Rapids: Eerdmans, 1996.
Lerner, Robert E., et al. *Western Civilizations: Their History and Their Culture*. 13th ed. New York: W. W. Norton, 1998.
Levine, Lee I. *Judaism and Hellenism in Antiquity: Conflict or Confluence*. Seattle: University of Washington Press, 1998.
Noth, Martin. *The History of Israel*. 2nd ed. London: Redwood, 1959.

Bibliography

Pearlman, Moshe. *The Maccabees*. London: Macmillan, 1973.
Provan, Iain, et al. *A Biblical History of Israel*. Louisville: Westminster John Knox, 2003.
Richardson, Peter. *Herod: King of the Jews and Friend of the Romans*. Minneapolis: Fortress, 1999.
Schiffman, Lawrence H. *Reclaiming the Dead Sea Scrolls: The History of Judaism, the Background of Christianity, the Lost Library of Qumran*. New York: Doubleday, 1995.
Soggin, J. Alberto. *The History of Ancient Israel*. Philadelphia: Westminster, 1985.
Vermes, Geza. *The True Herod*. London: Bloomsbury, 2014.

Index

Abilene, 81, 88
Abomination of Desolation, 28, 40, 47, 112
Abraham, xiii, 11, 66, 68, 122
Abram, xiii
Acra, 28, 30, 33–37, 39, 64
Actian Games, 61, 112
Actium, 49, 58, 60, 62
Acts, 67
Age of Reason, 115
agora, 62, 111
Agrippa I, 81, 87–88, 105–6
Agrippa II, 88, 90–92, 95, 107
Agrippa, Marcus, 65
Agrippias, 63–64
Albinus, Lucius, 92–94, 107
Alcimus, 32–34
Alexander the Great, 14–15, 17–19, 25, 40, 61, 99–100, 114
Alexander, Herod's son, 72–73, 76–77
Alexander, Tiberius, 88–89, 106
Alexandra II, 56–60, 103
Alexandria, 17, 50, 64, 86–87
Alexandrium, 46, 64
Altar of Burnt Offering, 68
Amathus, 42
Ambivius, Marcus, 84
amphitheater, 61, 63, 87, 112, 114
Ananel, 56–57
Ananias, 93
Ananus, 92, 109
Anthedon, 42
Antigonus, 42, 50–54, 56, 69

Antioch, 27, 30–32, 35, 38, 53, 65, 95
Antiochus III, 17–18
Antiochus IV, 27–30, 32, 39, 47, 100, 104, 112
Antiochus V, 31–32
Antiochus VI, 36, 38
Antiochus VII, 39, 41, 100
Antipas, 77–81, 85–87, 105
Antipater, 44, 48–50, 54, 76, 101
Antipater, Herod's son, 72–73, 75
Antipatris, 63–64
Antonia, 64–65, 67, 69, 75, 88–89, 95, 107–8, 111
Antony, Mark, 49–50, 52, 56–60, 64, 69, 101
Apollo, 21
Apollonia, 19
Aquinas, Thomas, 114
Arab, 58–59
Aramaic, 54
Archelaus, 77–83, 93, 105–7
Aretas, 44, 73–74
Aristobulus I, 42, 113
Aristobulus II, 43–48, 50, 113
Aristobulus III, 56–57, 59, 101
Aristobulus, Herod's son, 72–73, 76–77, 80
Aristotle, 2, 23–24
Ark of the Covenant, 68
Artaxerxes, 5, 7–9
Artaxerxes III, 13
Ascalon, 19, 65
Asia Minor, 1, 15, 18, 33, 58, 69
Askelon, 63

Index

Assyria, xiii, 4
Assyrians, 3–4
Athens, 2, 14, 62
Attica, 2
Augustus, 59, 62, 65, 69–70, 73–74, 76–77, 79–81, 84, 104
Aurantis, 59, 66, 73, 78, 80–81

Babylon, xiii, xv, 7, 16, 18, 51, 58, 67, 111
Bacchides, 33
Bacon, Francis, 115–16
Bactria, 16
Balas, 34–36, 39
Batanaea, 59, 63, 78, 80–81
Bathyra, 63
Battle of Actium, 57
Battle of Gaugamela, 16
Battle of Granicus, 15
Battle of Ipsis, 16
Battle of Issus, 15
Battle of Marathon, 2
Battle of Phillippi, 49
Battle of Platea, 2, 14
Battle of Salamis, 2
behaviorists, 116, 119–20
Belshazzar, 1, 3
Ben Sira, 26
Berenice, 72
Berytus, 64, 76, 87
Betharamphtha, 65, 80
Bethlehem, 65, 101, 104–5
Bickerman, Elias, 112, 114
Bloom, Allan, 122
Bogoras, 75
Book of Jubilees, 24
Book of Maccabees 26
Brutus, 49

Caesarea Maritima, 39, 62–63, 65–66, 70–71, 82, 84, 88–97, 106–8, 110
Caesarea Philippi, 80
Caligula, 80–81, 86–87, 94, 106
Cambyses, 1, 4
Canaan, xiii, 6, 11, 121
Canaanites, 5, 9
Capernaum, 110
Cappadocia, 33–34

Carthage, 18
Cassius, 49–50
Castobarus, 60, 66
Chaeronea, 14
Chalcis, 88
Chios, 64
Claudius, 87–88, 90
Cleopatra, 39, 50, 56–59, 64
Cleopatra, Herod's wife, 77–78
Cold War, 117
colonnade, 111
Coponius, 84–86, 106
Corinth, 21
Corinthian Gate, 68
Council of Elders, 16–17, 42–43
Court of Gentiles, 67–68, 71
Court of Israel, 67–68
Court of Priests, 67–68
Court of Women, 67–68
Croesus, 1–2
Cummanus, Ventidius, 89–90, 106
cupbearer, 7
Cypros, 64–65
Cyprus, 34
Cyrus, 1–4

Damascus, 45, 59, 63, 81
Darius, 1–4
Darius II, 12
Darius III, 12, 15
David, xiii, xv, 41, 43, 46, 54–55, 66, 68, 82, 104
Day of Atonement, 56, 68
Dead Sea, 12, 33, 41, 43, 52, 55, 64–65, 98
Decapolis, 47, 59, 96
Descartes, Rene, 115
Delphi, 21
Delian League, 14
Demetrius, 32–34
Demetrius II, 35–39, 41
Demetrius III, 43
Democritus, 21
Derrida, Jacques, 119–20
Deuteronomy, 113
Diodotus, 36
Doris, 77

Index

eagle, 75–76
Ecclesiasticus, 25
Edomites, 53
Egypt, 6, 16–17, 28, 35, 48, 53, 57–58, 66, 86, 97
Eleazar, 90
Enlightenment, 114–15, 117–20
Epicureanism, 24
Epicureans, 24
Epirus, 62
Esar-haddon, 4
Essenes, 46, 55, 74, 101
Euphrates River, 53
Exodus, 121
exodus, 6, 53
Ezra, xiv, 3, 5–6, 9–11, 99, 104, 113, 123

Fadus, Cuspus, 88–89, 106
Feast of Tabernacles, 56–57
Felix, Antonius, 90–93, 106, 108–9
Festival of Booths, 6
Festus, Porcius, 92, 109
First Roman War, xiv, xv, 82, 88, 105
First Temple, 67
Flaccus, 86
Florus, Gessius, 94–95, 107
Foucault, Michele, 118–19, 120

Gaba, 63
Gabinius, 46–48
Gadara, 20, 42
Gaius, 86
Galatians, 64
Galilee, 42–43, 47–50, 52, 54, 65, 78, 80–81, 85, 95–96, 101, 103, 110
Gallus, Cestius, 95–96
Gaul, 81
Gaulantis, 42
Gaza, 42, 63
Gazara, 38, 47
Genesis, 121
Gerasa, 20
Germans, 64
Gilead, 42
Gill, Ross, ix
Gischala, 96–97
Glaphyra, 72
Grant, Michael, xiv, 104

Gratius, Valerius, 84
Greece, 2–3, 9, 66, 111
Grenz, Stanley, 116, 120

Haggai, 3–4
Halys River, 1
Hasidim, 24, 30–32, 42, 113
Hasmonean, 30, 38, 44–47, 50, 55–58, 60, 63, 67, 69, 100–102, 112–13
Hasmoneans, 29, 39–40, 46–47, 55–56, 75–76, 100–101, 113–14, 122
Hebron, 66, 71
Helena, 88
Hellenism, xv, 19, 24, 27, 61, 100, 102, 114
Herod, 48–51, 53–60, 62–72, 75–76, 78–82, 84, 87, 91, 95, 101, 103–5, 106, 110, 111
Herodias, 80–81
Herodium, 63, 70, 78, 88
Herodotus, 2
Heshbon, 63
Hezekiah's Pool, 65
Hillel, 55
hippodrome, 61–63, 77, 112, 114
Holocaust, 117
Holy of Holies, 46, 68
Holy Place, 68
Hyrcania, 64
Hyrcanus I, 38–42, 44, 53, 62, 100–101, 111
Hyrcanus II, 43–52, 54, 56, 58–59, 101, 103, 113

Idumea, 38, 44, 47, 53, 62, 65–66, 78, 80, 87, 97, 100, 105, 113
Illyrium, 49
Ionia, 15
Iraq, 16
Irbil, 16
Isaac, xiii, 68
Isthmian Games, 2
Iturea, 59
Itureans, 42, 59

Jabbok River, 64
Jacob, xiii, 66
Jaffa, 37
James, 92, 108–9

141

Index

Jamnia, 86, 98
Jannai, 42–44, 46, 53, 55, 64, 101–2, 113
Jason, 28
Jehoiachin, 3
Jericho, 47, 56–57, 63–65, 97, 110
Jeroboam, xiii
Jerusalem, xiii, 3–9, 12–13, 15, 19–20, 27, 29, 31–34, 36–37, 39–41, 43, 45–51, 54, 60–62, 64–66, 72, 76–79, 82–84, 86, 88, 90, 93, 95–99, 106–9, 110–11, 113
Jeshua, 4
Jesus, 85–86, 92, 108–9
Joazar, 83
Johanan, 38
John, 67, 121
John the Baptist, 80–81
John of Gischala, 86, 98
Jonathan, 33–40, 42
Jonathan, high priest, 91
Joppa, 19, 48, 52
Jordan River, 17, 41–42
Joseph, xiii
Joseph, husband of Mary, 68
Josephus, Flavius, 15, 66, 80, 84, 89, 92–93, 96
Joshua, 6
Jotapata, 96
Judas, Gaulantis radical, 83–84, 89, 94, 106–7
Judea, xiii, 1–2, 7, 9–10, 12–13, 16, 18, 19–20, 26–27, 32, 34–39, 41, 43, 45–53, 62, 64–65, 70, 72, 75, 78, 80, 82, 85, 87–88, 90, 92, 94, 98, 100–102, 105–8, 110, 112
Julia, 80
Julius Caesar, 48–49, 101

Khirbet Qumran, 55

Lake Gennesaret, 80
League of Nations, 117
Leah, 66
Lebanon, 88
Lepidus, 49
Levites, 7, 13
Luke, 68

Lydia, 1
Lyotard, Jean Francois, 120
Lysias, 30–33
Lysias, Tribune, 108–9

McDowell, James, xi
Maccabaeus, Judas, 30–33, 37, 40, 45, 47, 67
Maccabean, 45–46, 100, 104
Maccabees, xv, 10, 30–33, 46, 100
Macedon, 14, 16
Machaeras, 98
Machpelah Caves, 66
Magnesia, 18
Malpech Caves, 71
Malthace, 77
Mamillah Pool, 65
Mamre, 66, 71
Marcellus, 86
Mariamne, 50, 56, 58–60, 72, 103
Marisa, 20
Mark, 80
Marulla, 94
Marullius, 86
Mary, 68
Masada, 52, 64–65, 70, 98
Mattathias, 29–30, 40
Matthew, 80
Matthew, Capernaum tax collector, 110
Menelaus, 28, 30–32, 112
Mesopotamia, 1
metanarrative, 120–21
Mithridates, 39
Moab, 42
modernism, 114, 118
modernist, 120
Modin, 29
Messiah, 85
Moses, xiii, xiv, 5–7, 10, 53–54, 86, 113, 123
Mount Carmel, 43, 65
Mount Gerizim, 41, 86
Mount of Olives, 91

Nabataeans, 42–43, 45, 52–53, 63, 69, 73, 80–81, 88
Nazarene, 108

Index

Nebuchadnezzar, 3, 7, 67
Nehemiah, xiv, 7–12, 89, 104, 113, 123
Nero, 92–93, 96–97
Newton, Isaac, 115–16
Nicolaus of Damascus, 74, 76, 80
Nicopolis, 60
Nietzsche, Friedrich, 117–20
Noth, Martin, xiv, 47, 94

Obodas, 73
Octavian, 49, 57–61, 70, 101
Olympia, 66
Olympiad, 20, 61
Onias II, 39

Palestine, xiv, 1, 12, 15–19, 45, 47–49, 56, 63, 97, 99
Panias, 59, 65, 80
Parthians, 30–32, 38, 41, 50–52, 100–101
Passover, 56, 79, 85, 89, 110
Paul, 91–92, 108–9
Pella, 20, 96
Peloponnesian War, 22
Pentecost, 56, 79
Pente Komai, 63
Perea, 47–48, 63, 65, 75, 78, 80–81
Pericles, 2
Pergamum, 34
Persepolis, 1, 16
Persia, xiii, 1–3, 9, 14, 16, 30
Persian Empire, 15, 17, 99
Persians, XV, 16, 18, 99, 100
Petra, 74
Petronius, Publius, 86–87, 94
phalanx, 15
Pharisees, 42–44, 46, 54–55, 74–75, 85, 92, 94–96, 98, 101, 108–9
Pharsalus, 48–49
Phasael, 48, 50–52, 63
Phasaelis, 63–64
Pheroras, 74–75, 77
Philadelphia, 20
Philip, Herod's son, 77–81, 87, 105
Philip, imperial regent, 31
Philip V, Macedonian king, 14, 18
Pilate, Pontius, 84–85, 105–6, 110
Piraeus, 62

Plato, 2, 23–24
Pompey, 45–49, 62, 101
Pool of Israel, 65
portico, 87, 111
Poseidon, 21
postmodernism, 114, 118, 122–23
postmodernist, 119, 120–21
Praetorian Guard, 87
prefect, 82–83, 86, 94
procurator, 82, 89, 91–92, 98, 101, 106, 108
Province Beyond the River, xiii, 1, 3–5, 7–8, 12, 89
Ptolemais, 19, 35, 37, 42, 63, 96
Ptolemies, XV, 16–18, 27, 34, 40
Ptolemy I, 16–17
Ptolemy IV, 34
Punic Wars, 18
Pythagorus, 22
Pythian Games, 21

Qudratus, Ummidus, 90
Quirinius, 83, 89, 93, 106, 110

Rachael, 66
Ragaba, 43
Raphia, 42
Rehoboam, xiii
Renaissance, 114–15
Rhodes, 58–59, 64, 66, 69, 108
Richardson, Peter, 62, 69
Roman, 45–48, 53, 58, 69–70, 75, 81–83, 85, 89, 95–98, 101, 104–5, 108, 110, 114
Roman Empire, xv, 45, 47–49, 53, 60, 62, 70, 72, 74, 100, 102
Rome, 18, 34–34, 37, 45, 47–50, 52, 55, 57, 59–61, 65–66, 69, 72–74, 77, 79, 81, 86–88, 90, 92, 95, 97–98, 101, 102, 104–5, 107, 109–10
Royal Porch, 67
Royal Road, 1
Rufus, Annius, 84

Sadducees, 42, 44, 46, 54–55, 92, 94, 101–3, 109
Salome, 60, 72, 75, 77–78

143

Index

Salome, Alexandra, 42–44, 55, 100–102
Salome, daughter of Antipas and Herodias, 80
Samaria, 4, 13, 17, 19, 37–38, 41, 43, 47, 60–62, 64, 69, 78, 80, 86–87, 90, 97, 105–6, 113
Samaritans, 4, 81, 86, 90
Sanballat, 8–9
Sanctuary, 67–68
Sanhedrin, 49, 83, 92, 96, 98, 109, 113
Sarah, 66
Sardis, 1
Saturninus, 73
Scaurus, 45
Schiffman, Lawrence, 55
Scholasticism, 114
Scythopolis, 19, 96
Sea of Galilee, 59, 66
Sebaste, 62–64, 66, 69–71
Second Chronicles, 3, 68
Second Commandment, 75
Second Nabataean War, 73
Second Temple, 5, 19, 55, 62, 66–67, 113–14, 122
Second Timothy, 10
Seleucid Empire, 35, 38–39, 45, 47, 99, 101
Seleucids, xv, 16–18, 40, 45, 47, 99, 113
Seleucus, 16
Seleucus IV, 18
Sepphoris, 47, 65, 80
Sextus, 49
Shammai, 55
Shechem, 19, 41, 43
Sheep Pool, 65
Sheshbazzar, 3–5
Shetharbozenai, 4
sicarii, 93
Sider, John, ix
Sidetes, 39
Sidon, 63
Silent Years, xv, 10–12, 82, 99, 104–5, 111
Silo, 52
Simon, 35–40, 112–13
Simon bar Giora, 97–98
Simonides, 20
Sinai, xiii, 6–7, 11
Silva, Flavius, 98

Socrates, 2, 22–23
Soggin, Alberto, xiv
Solomon, xiii, xv, 43, 46, 59, 92, 104
Solomon's Pool, 65
Solomon's Porch, 67
Sophism, 22
Sophists, 22–23
Sosius, 53
Stephen, 108–9
stoa, 64, 71, 111
Stoicism, 24
Stoics, 24
Strato's Tower, 62, 91
Struthion Pool, 65
Supreme Council, 98
Susa, 1, 7–9, 16
Syllaeus, 73–74
Synagogue of the Freedmen, 109
Syria, 16, 27, 32–33, 36, 38–39, 41, 43, 45, 47–48, 50–52, 57–58, 77, 79–81, 83, 95, 101

Table of Showbread, 68
Tattenai, 4–5
Tekoa, 33
temple, 3–7, 29, 46–47, 71, 75–76, 82, 97–99, 103, 106–8, 111–12, 114
Temple of Pythian Apollo, 66
Temple of Roma, 62–63, 65
Ten Commandments, 6, 11, 68
Thales, 21
theater, 61, 63, 87, 112
Tholomy, 88
Thracians, 64
Thucydides, 2
Tiberias, 80
Tiberius, 80–81, 84, 87
Titus, 96–98
Tobiah, 8–9
Torah, 24, 26, 29, 55, 61, 112
Trachonitis, 59, 73, 78, 80–81
Tripolis, 63
Tryphon, 36–39, 41
Tunisia, 18
Turkey, 1, 64
Tyre, 15, 64, 69

Index

Ulatha, 59
Utica, 20

Varus, 77, 79
Veil of the Temple, 68
Ventidius, 52
Vespasian, 96–97
Vitellus, 86

World War I, 117
World War II, 117

Yarmuk River, 42, 83
Yom Kipur, 68

Xerxes, 2

Zacchaeus, 110
Zadok, 27, 54, 56
Zealots, 90, 94, 96–97, 107
Zechariah, 4
Zeno, 24
Zenodorus, 59
Zerubbabel, 3–5, 8–9
Zerubbabel's temple, 67
Zeus, 21, 28

www.ingramcontent.com/pod-product-compliance
Lightning Source LLC
Chambersburg PA
CBHW050823160426
43192CB00010B/1873